Also by Robert Trumbull

THE RAFT

SILVERSIDES

AS I SEE INDIA

By Robert Trumbull

WILLIAM SLOANE ASSOCIATES
New York . . . 1956

Published simultaneously in the Dominion of Canada
by George J. McLeod Limited, Toronto.
Printed in the United States of America.
Library of Congress Catalog Card Number: 56-6629

To Jean, who lived it.

Contents

MAPS

(Courtesy of *The New York Times.*)

AS I SEE INDIA

1

Blood, Sweat, and Tear Gas

They called him "First-wave" Jones in the Pacific. Neither shot nor shell nor malarious jungle stayed his steps on beachhead after beachhead along the island-dotted trail from Guadalcanal to Tokyo Bay. At war's end George Jones was assigned to India, and it took just eleven months for the climate and the germs to lay him low.

I got a hurry-up cable to fly to New Delhi from Singapore, where I was then stationed, so George could be evacuated at once. He had a variety of illnesses: typhoid, pneumonia, phlebitis, and an embolism, one after the other and sometimes overlapping. I was to take over for a couple of weeks, pending the arrival of another staff man from New York. But when word got around the office of *The New York Times* what had happened to George, no one was anxious to come to India. As for me, well, I was there!

The ordinary assignment to India for most foreign correspondents, like diplomats, is two years. After the second hellish summer in New Delhi, I mentioned this casually to my managing editor, the late Edwin L. James, adding the information that a British colleague had died not long before of heat stroke, and that this man's predecessor, in a fit of hot weather despondency, had shot himself. But, I said, I shouldn't mind staying on, although it would be nice if the office sent me out an air conditioner. Everything I had said was true, but

I hadn't expected any serious reaction until Mr. James cabled back, "What size air conditioner?"

And I stayed in India seven and a half years. In that time I was to see India evolve from a nation of doubtful hopes, born in uncertainty and bloodshed, into the most stable country in Asia and a voice of strong moral power in world affairs.

In my early days, like all newcomers to India, I was intensely preoccupied with the elementary problem of trying to be reasonably comfortable in one of the world's most trying climates.

There aren't many places with heat like North India. The summer lasts eight months, from early March to late October. March and October are tolerable; the air conditioning goes on in April and goes off at the end of September. The four "winter" months are grand, with pleasant, tangy days that are perfect for outdoor pursuits, and bracing nights when an open fire is pleasant. Some time in March, suddenly, you are walking along the street, enjoying a sort of semi-tropical spring, when the merest breath of overheated air touches your skin like a fleeting tongue of flame. This is the first flicker of the *loo*, the terrible, dust-laden hot wind that will soon turn the North Indian plain into a parched inferno for most of April, May and June.

To a veteran, it does not seem really hot until the temperature gets to about 98 degrees Fahrenheit. At the height of the summer it will be near 120 in New Delhi at midday, and still over 100 most of the night. There is no surcease, no hope, for the masses who have no air conditioning and cannot afford to flee, like the wealthier classes, to the hills.

In British times, New Delhi closed down on April 15. Three days later the entire government arrived at Simla, 7,000 feet high in the approaches to the Himalayas. There they stayed until October 15, when the trek down began. In the intervening months New Delhi, which was built strictly as a capital city separate from the adjacent "Old" Delhi, was all but deserted. The annual moving process was halted by the war. Afterward, the Indians' own government abandoned the custom for various reasons. One reason, I think, was that the British did it. Also, it was considered unnational to shrink from the hardships of climate that the bulk of the population could not escape. And, of course, moving the entire official establishment to Simla and back every year was an expensive process hard for a democratic government to justify. The only argument in its favor was that working in the cool hills promoted efficiency. But there isn't much efficiency anyway in the Indian government.

After several years the government air-conditioned the Houses of Parliament, though some of the members found the coolness uncomfortable and brought light shawls to the chamber. Cooling was gradually introduced into the offices of the most important officials, but Prime Minister Jawaharlal Nehru doesn't like it for himself. Most Indians, lacking expensive air conditioning, avail themselves of the cheap *khus-khus tattie,* possibly the oldest system of air conditioning on earth and whose principle undoubtedly suggested the modern machine. The *tattie* is a thick screen woven of the fragrant *khus-khus* grass, and placed in doors and windows. A water pipe arrangement, or, more often, a boy with a pail and teacup, keeps the screen wet. The burning *loo,* blowing through, picks up moisture, and this drops the temperature inside the room five or ten degrees, besides filling the air with a delicate, refreshing fragrance.

Come June with the monsoon rains, and the *khus-khus tattie* is no good, for the air then has too much moisture. The mercury plummets to the nineties, but the humidity is near saturation. However, the first monsoon rain in Delhi is an occasion for celebration. Indians undress and stand in the downpour, laving their skin to rid it of the inevitable prickly heat, for which there is no cure but a trip to the cool hills. But sustained heat with high humidity means that the irritating rash will soon be back again, for the monsoon time is by far the sweatiest season.

At formal parties, still held in stubborn defiance of the climate, not only one's shirt but one's white dinner jacket will soak clear through (when I have had the opportunity, I have slipped to my room and changed my shirt and jacket twice in one evening). The British introduced a welcome summer costume still seen at gatherings that are not too, too formal: black evening trousers, plain white shirt with black bow tie and cummerbund—no jacket. (In Bengal there is a variation, that makes no sense to me, consisting of ordinary black dinner jacket but with lightweight white trousers.)

Life in India used to be a lot more formal than it is today. In former times the British wore wool at important functions in the middle of summer. An amusing concession to the heat used to occur at Belvedere, the British Viceroy's residence when the capital was in Calcutta. The guest arrived in formal black. The Viceroy, meeting his guest at the door, would inquire if he wouldn't like to change to something more comfortable. Well, as it happened, the guest would reply, his bearer had just chanced to bring along a white coat. Then, punctilio having been satisfied, the guest would take off his black coat, hand it to his bearer, and put on the white one. The ladies, then as now, were the only persons dressed sensibly for a hot climate.

When I arrived in India, and for several years thereafter, one needed more dinner jackets, white and black, than business suits. All summer, no one wears a coat and necktie except when calling on a *very* important official, or when invited to a luncheon (in which case, quite often, the gentlemen are invited to remove their coats). But after 6 P.M., any invitation meant a dinner jacket, unless it was specifically stated that the occasion was to be "informal," and this seldom happened, even for a small party consisting entirely of close friends meeting in the apartment of one of them.

This began to change in about 1951, as more and more Americans came to New Delhi. Many of them, either through unawareness or to save weight in their airplane luggage, were unequipped with dinner jackets, and their hosts, to put the travelers at ease, also appeared in business suits. Chester Bowles, America's most informal ambassador, was the first top-ranking diplomat to break down the dress rules; he appeared in "black tie" only on such special occasions as the annual "national day" receptions of the various embassies and the Indian government. This quickly became the custom, and now Delhi-ites, barring a few dyed-in-the-wool British types, no longer feel impelled to get into evening wear just to drop into a night club for a casual dance and a drink with their wives, and most invitation cards bear the notation, "Informal."

It was easier, and certainly less strain on the clothing budget for men, in the old days when there was no question but what one would "dress" for any occasion after six. Now it is often uncertain whether one is expected to wear "black tie" or not to the type of function that might be either way. Nothing really has been gained by the new informality in India, for in that climate one ordinarily bathes and changes before dinner anyway, and the lightweight material of the modern summer dinner jacket is as comfortable as any other suit.

Indians, of course, never have to worry about "what to wear," for the "national" dress—one never says "native"—has always been acceptable. In fact, however, some British-educated Indians of the official and professional classes were inclined to be as meticulous as their mentors, or more so if possible, in the matter of evening dress. Some of this stratum of Indian society, even more than the old-line British and the stuffier Americans, were disapproving of Chester Bowles's defiance of convention.

At just about the same time that the Americans, led by Mr. Bowles, were breaking down the "black tie" custom, Mr. Nehru became so preoccupied with the vagaries of Indian dress that he made the matter a minor national issue. In the first place, the Prime Minister seemed to consider the wearing of Western evening costume somehow unpatriotic, at least in India. He himself, always in his own country and abroad in recent years, wears the *achkan*, a high-necked coat, and the tight-legged *churidar* trousers (often incorrectly called jodhpurs, which are slightly different). He also sometimes wears his ancestral Kashmiri costume, which substitutes a vestlike garment for the *achkan*.

Mr. Nehru became quite thoughtful on the subject of Indian dress at one point several years ago. He issued a long memorandum to government officers in which he set down his musings on the broad subject of the history and mutations of Indian costume. At this time Mr. Nehru made it an official regulation that the *achkan* and *churidar* should be the accepted dress for Indian diplomats and others on formal occasions.

With this costume Mr. Nehru invariably wears the white cap affected by members of the ruling Congress party, usually called the "Gandhi cap," a misnomer because Gandhi never wore it. This headgear becomes Mr. Nehru: it conceals his baldness completely and thus makes him look younger. Sikhs, of course, wear the turban at all times in public, as required by their religion, and some Punjabis, Marathas, Madrasis and others wear their own distinctive turbans with striking effect. Western headgear would look a little ridiculous with the *achkan* and *churidar*.

There was some satirical grumbling when Mr. Nehru's dress decree was published. Some Indians wondered aloud and in print if they weren't being regimented a bit too much. But except for the class that aped the British in all things, it had long been the custom to wear the smart and comfortable *achkan*, or the longer and wide-skirted *sherwani*, on all dress-up occasions. It could be either formal or informal, and Indians said it was more comfortable than the Western coat and tie. Often ordinary black or white trousers, either plain or satin-striped, were worn with contrasting upper garment:

black top and white trousers for winter, white top and black trousers for summer.

Indian women, both in their homeland and abroad, invariably wear the *sari* or the wide trousers and blouse (*salwar kameez*), with graceful *dopatta* or scarf, affected in the Punjab and Sind. Almost the only exception for women is sports wear, for which modern Indian females have adopted slacks, shorts and jodhpurs, but it is still common to see females competing in tennis, running and jumping and field hockey in the restricting *sari* and *salwar kameez*, which must inhibit their speed and freedom of movement.

Generally speaking, an Indian woman seen in a dress can be taken to be an Anglo-Indian Christian, or a Goan. But more Indian children, in the cities at least, appear to wear Western dress than not. Nehru made some pungent remarks on this once when he handed out diplomas at a Delhi school and found most of the graduates in Western suits.

Some Indians thought that even such a popular idol as Nehru may have gone too far in trifling with personal matters when he set out to dictate what the ladies should wear at work in government offices. For the female, he decreed *sari* of plain, quiet color, with no wide border, and the midriff completely covered. More often than not, the *choli*, the tight, short-sleeved upper garment worn under the graceful fold of the *sari*, is hardly more than a covering for the brassière, if any, leaving the stomach bare almost to the navel and sometimes beyond. The far from unpleasing effect is to make it appear that Indian women have the most prominent breasts and longest midriffs in the world, which may be true.

One of the compensations of living in India is the extraordinary beauty of the women (unfortunately, many of those who go abroad do not seem to be up to the home standard) and their colorful dress. The Indian woman's graceful carriage—which in the peasant, at least, may come from the custom of carrying burdens on the head—is certainly unexcelled, and may be the reason why only an Indian woman really looks right in some types of *sari*.

Mr. Nehru hasn't expressed himself publicly, so far as I know, on that abomination among all male dress, the *dhoti*. This is the garment, worn in most of the country, consisting of a length of homespun cotton cloth wound about the waist and pulled up between the legs and tucked in. In the most prevalent type of *dhoti*—styles varying slightly in different provinces—walking exposes the bare shanks with a ridiculous effect made even more esthetically objectionable when the wearer has on Western socks and garters. The *kurta*, or shirt, hangs outside in a sloppy fashion that is not so objectionable with a *dhoti*, for nothing could make a *dhoti* look worse than it normally does; but many Indians tend to cling to this method of wearing an ordinary long-tailed shirt, with Western trousers, making an appearance which to foreign eyes is slovenly and absurd. I do not hesitate to express the opinion that the average Indian man in the street, unshaven, unkempt, and dressed in his ordinary fashion, is the sloppiest individual in the world.

Slovenly attire and filth in the streets, being so obvious, are the first things a newcomer notices in India. Arriving as I did in June, I was also hit literally in the face by that other great conversational gambit concerning India, the heat. As the plane wheeled before the terminal building at Willingdon Airport, it was broiling inside. But out on the tarmac it was even hotter. George hobbled out on a cane to meet me, and my first words to him were, "My God, George, is it always this hot in Delhi?"

I had just come from Singapore and way points in Southeast Asia, and had lived south of the Tropic of Cancer for fourteen years, but the day of my arrival in Delhi I got a touch of heat sickness, and spent the first night sharing George's air-conditioned hospital room. But one can get used to anything; the next seven summers didn't seem so bad, probably because I was able to find occasional excuses to go to the hills, and after two years I had the air conditioner.

History was being made in New Delhi that week. Lord Louis Mountbatten, the last Viceroy, had just presented the Congress party and the Moslem League the final British proposal for freeing India. This was the historic partition plan whereby the country was to be divided into two Dominions, Hindu India and Moslem Pakistan. Formal ratification was still due from the Pakistan party, the Moslem League headed by Mohammed Ali Jinnah. The League was to hold its meeting in the ballroom of the Hotel Imperial, and it fell to me to cover the story. In so doing I was almost hit in the head with a shovel, just missed being pushed over a second-story banister, and was slightly tear-gassed. What an introduction to India, I thought, and hoped my replacement would arrive soon. A lot of blood, sweat and tear gas was to flow before I said good-by to India, in a much different frame of mind.

2

Children of the Dust

My first news assignment in India raised doubts as to the self-avowed nonviolence of Indians. And after watching the events of the following turbulent months, the claim of Indians that they achieved their independence bloodlessly seemed preposterous. The transfer of power was accompanied by one of the most atrocious slaughters in modern history. The conflict was not between the Indians and the British, though there had been plenty of that in decades gone by to belie the Indian claim to nonviolence, but between Indian Moslems and Hindus and Sikhs.

As it happened, my first encounter with violence in India found Moslems fighting Moslems. Islam has many sects, and to this day in India one occasionally finds Shias rising against Sunnis. The affair I witnessed early in June, 1947, was not religious, however, but political. It was a small matter, on the whole, but it turned out to be indicative of the Indian temperament when aroused.

Mohammed Ali Jinnah, president of the Moslem League, had summoned his lieutenants to an evening meeting in the grand ballroom of the Hotel Imperial to ratify the Mountbatten partition plan. The ratification was formal. But not all Moslems in India were in favor of partition, and one of the organized opposition groups decided to demonstrate at the Moslem League gathering. These were the Khaksars, one of those odd, semimystic movements that rise from time to time in India, make their mark, and fade away like evanescent political parties.

The Khaksars, or "Children of the Dust," were significant of their time in that they gave fanatic expression to the nationalism of some Indian Moslems, as opposed to the "two-nation theory" that created Pakistan. They were, in a smaller way, the Moslem counterpart of the extreme Hindu nationalist Rashtrya Swayamsevak Sangh (National Volunteer Corps), or RSS, which is still a force in India.

Both the Khaksars and the RSS were militant youth organizations with uniforms, and exulting in military drill and discipline. The Khaksars had as their emblem the spade or garden shovel, called *belcha* in Urdu, which they glorified almost like an article of worship. One of their members wrote a poem in Urdu listing one hundred uses for the *belcha:* as a weapon, cooking utensil, digging tool, walking staff, pillow, and so on.

As Jinnah and the other Moslem League leaders were gathering in the second-floor ballroom, thirty or forty Khaksars, with bright-edged *belcha* over their shoulders, rushed the stairs. It was not known what they intended to do. A platoon of red-turbaned Delhi police leaped to the crowded stairway, swinging their *lathi,* or long, weighted clubs. Several reporters, including myself, were caught in the crush, and it looked for a few minutes as if we would be accidentally pushed through the banister by the weight of the struggling bodies, or cut in the head by one of the waggling, sharpened *belcha.* The police exploded a couple of tear-gas grenades, which caused everyone including the press to push toward the exits, coughing and weeping.

This was about the last time the Khaksars made any splash in the papers, and the organization was soon dying and forgotten. But the incident in the hotel was a dramatic introduction to the conflicts that rendered the subcontinent of India asunder. There are numerous provincial and factional interests whose activities from time to time have served to demonstrate the country's lack of homogeneity. Among these, the conflict that has had the most tragic influence on Indian history has been the ancient enmity between Hindus and Moslems. It was this animosity, dating back nearly a thousand years, that seems now to have made the creation of Pakistan inevitable, even though the geographical contours of that country, bisected by a thousand miles of Indian territory, appear to violate all political and economic sense.

The faith of Mohammed, carried by Arab seamen, touched only the maritime fringes of India until the raiding hordes of Mahmud of Ghazni, a fierce Afghan chieftain, swept through the Punjab at the beginning of the eleventh century. Mahmud sowed seeds of hatred that still flourish.

Mahmud of Ghazni descended upon the North Indian plains seventeen times, sweeping down from his Afghan retreat in the fall, retiring in the spring, laden with booty. It wasn't his robberies that bothered the Hindus so much, but rather his hobby of despoiling temples and breaking idols. His destruction of Somnath, a particularly sacred temple of Shiva in Kathiawar in northwest India (now Saurashtra), has never been forgotten. One of the first projects of the newly free India was the restoration of Somnath, and the occasion of the rededication, attended by leading Hindus, had more than ordinary significance.

The forays of Mahmud began an era of Moslem conquests in India that lasted until the rise of British power. The Mogul Empire, which in the days of Akbar the Great (1556-1605) included all but the southern part of India, endured nominally until the capture and exile of the last Emperor, Bahadur Shah, by the victorious British at Delhi at the end of the Sepoy Mutiny of 1857. (The Indians call this uprising the First War for Independence; it may be fortunate for India that it did not succeed, for a long period of backwardness and internecine warfare might have ensued, instead of which the British in the following ninety years fostered the building of the modern state that India is today.)

In the period of Moslem rule, about a quarter of the population of India embraced the religion of the Prophet. Wholesale conversions, sometimes to escape caste distinctions and particularly the stigma of untouchability, outraged Hindu feelings and contributed to the animosity felt toward Moslems to this day. Islam naturally became strongest along the traditional invasion path from the Khyber Pass across North India to East Bengal, but the religion spread all over India in the wake of Moslem conquest. Only in the Western provinces of Baluchistan, Sind and the Northwest Frontier and Kashmir, western Punjab, eastern Bengal, and Sylhet were the Moslems in a numerical majority over Hindus, however. These are the territories that formed Pakistan in 1947.

In ordinary daily contacts, Hindus and Moslems can get along quite well. Many Hindus and Moslems are fast friends, and during the 1947 partition riots in Delhi I knew personally of Hindus who sheltered Moslems against the vengeful bands who were bent on slaughtering them. The same thing happened in Pakistan, where some Moslems hid Hindus and Sikhs and helped them to escape to India. But over the long period, the relationship has been marked by sustained deep-seated enmity which often broke out, and does even today from time to time, as a result of some trivial incident.

The classic examples of incidents giving rise to bloody strife, repeated countless times, concern Moslems killing cows, which are sacred to Hindus, or cutting branches from the holy *peepul* tree to make way for processions with portable shrines. The Hindus sometimes offended Moslem sensibilities by taking clangorous processions past a mosque at prayer time, or it might be some instance of personal discrimination that aroused Moslem feelings and resulted in a riot.

Of more importance, perhaps, is the fact that Hinduism and Islam are not only widely disparate religions, but also encompass two incompatible social systems. The separateness of the Hindu social order from all others is recognized in legislation of the Indian Parliament since freedom, in new laws of marriage, divorce and so on that explicitly apply only to Hindus and the related communities of Sikhs, Jains and Buddhists. These laws do not affect Moslems, Parsis, Christians and Jews in India, whose ways of life are respected as being different, although the Republic of India is a secular state in which all are supposed to be equal under the law.

Hindus charge that the British deliberately exploited religious cleavages on the "divide and rule" principle. It is said that Moslems were made unduly conscious of their Islamic entity by the establishment of separate electorates and in many other ways, notably the reservation of a certain percentage of places in the services for the minority (all this applied to other minorities, too, such as the Untouchables). The British defense is that without special considerations the Moslems would have been hopelessly swamped by the more numerous and cleverer Hindus.

Communal cleavages were perpetually exacerbated by economic imbalances between Moslems and Hindus, in which the Moslem was usually the underdog. The Hindus, broadly speaking, included most of the landowners, bankers and merchants, while the Moslems were the cultivators and poor artisans. The Hindu moneylender, too, has brought ill will to his race and religion wherever he exists. In these circumstances, the Hindu's refusal to intermarry, or even sit at the same table, with non-Hindus lent point to the contention of Moslem League leaders that the Indian Mussulman's political salvation lay in separate nationhood.

Nevertheless, it was not until relatively late in the all-Indian struggle for independence that Moslems began to think of carving out their own state. The great Moslem political leaders of India, including the "father of Pakistan," Mohammed Ali Jinnah, had earlier been associated with the Indian National Congress, and had worked for a free India, undivided, in which Hindus and Moslems would live amicably under one government. The word "Pakistan," meaning

"Land of the Pure," did not gain currency until 1940.

But it was in 1937 that the Congress itself sealed the doom of an undivided India, by shutting out the Moslem League from participation in the governments of certain provinces where Moslems, though not in a majority numerically, had polled sizable votes. It was argued that the Congress, as the majority party, had no obligation to form a coalition government taking in a minority party. But such had been the Moslems' understanding, and it was at this point that Jinnah and others became convinced that Mussulmans in a united India would forever be a minority at the mercy of the Hindus. After that, there was no orderly way for the British to hand over sovereignty without recognizing two governments.

It was the obligation of the colonial power to leave a stable native regime. Very early in the history of the British in India, Viceroys had acknowledged that Britain's crowning achievement in the East would be the transfer of government to a worthy Indian state.

Lord Louis Mountbatten formally presented the partition plan on June 3, 1947, and it was accepted by both the Congress and the Moslem League. The Dominion of India was to consist of the former provinces of British India that were predominantly Hindu. The predominantly Moslem provinces were to form Pakistan. There were several doubtful areas, in which plebiscites were held, and actual boundaries were delineated by a commission comprised of two Pakistanis, two Indians, and a British chairman, Sir Cyril Radcliffe. The "Radcliffe Awards" in many instances have never been unqualifiedly accepted by either side, and minor adjustments have continued.

The Pakistanis are bitter about Mountbatten's haste in pushing through the physical partition. The last Viceroy set a deadline of August 15, 1947, for completing the immense task of laying out boundaries, dividing all assets down to typewriters and pens, parceling out the Army between the two sides, allocating railway cars, and so on. It was an impossible job to do in seventy-two days, and not even Mountbatten and his exceptionably able staff were equal to it. India and Pakistan are still squabbling over ownership of military stores and other materials left on one side or the other on the partition day. Since the seat of the British Indian government was in New Delhi, the Indian side had the advantage of inheriting a going establishment, whereas in Karachi, designated as Pakistan's capital, for months after the turnover high officials lacked office space and even writing materials.

Mr. Jinnah, in an interview he granted me in Karachi some months later, blamed Mountbatten's impatience to accomplish the partition for the devastating religious warfare that broke out immediately after August 15. That sad chapter will be a blot forever on the history of the two new states and, if Jinnah was right, also put an indelible smirch on the proud record of the British in India. Jinnah said Mountbatten could have prevented the slaughter, which took a million lives and uprooted twelve million persons from their ancestral homes, if he had acted on warnings.

Whether or not the British participate in blood guilt, it is obvious that the physical task of partition was far from complete when Lord Louis, at ceremonies in Karachi and New Delhi, formally handed over sovereignty for the British Crown on the appointed date. And the ensuing holocaust resurrected old hatreds and created new bitternesses that are likely to poison relationships between the two new states for at least a generation.

It is yet another question whether Hindus will ever relinquish the idea of a unified India, which would mean the obliteration of Pakistan; and whether Moslems of the more fanatical sort will ever forget that the crescent flag of Islam once flew from the Red Fort of Shah Jehan in Delhi. These questions are the concern not alone of India and Pakistan, but of all nations, for so long as the two neighbors are on bad terms there is danger for the peace of Asia and the world.

3

A Train to Lahore

MOHAMMED ALI JINNAH, IN WHAT WAS SAID TO HAVE BEEN A sudden change of mind, killed Lord Mountbatten's idea of being Governor-General of both India and Pakistan at the same time. The Indians were willing to retain Lord Louis as titular head of the state during the shakedown period, for Nehru and other Congress leaders had immense confidence in his judgment. Jinnah did not feel the same; he apparently believed that Mountbatten, having been Viceroy in New Delhi and being close to Nehru, would lean toward the Indian side in any dispute. In any case, Jinnah argued, it was a human and constitutional impossibility for one individual to represent the views of two opposed governments. In this respect, Jinnah may have underestimated Mountbatten's capabilities. Lord Louis, no doubt, as a dual Governor-General would have conceived it his mission to arbitrate the quarrels that immediately arose between the two new Dominions, if he had had equal responsibility to both. Possibly it was with this in mind that Mountbatten tackled the improbable task of effecting the partition in seventy-two days with such aplomb. His tenure as the simultaneous head of both states would, in effect, have continued the process of division that terminated, prematurely and disastrously, on August 15.

Mr. Jinnah as a Governor-General was unique in the constitutional structure of the British Commonwealth of Nations. The Governor-General is appointed by the British sovereign on advice of the Prime Minister, who in turn is advised by the cabinet of the Commonwealth state concerned. The Governor-General is nominally the personal representative of the sovereign, and plays about the same role in the government of a Dominion that the British monarch does in that of the United Kingdom. Normally he has no powers beyond those delegated to him by his Parliament; he signs bills and other documents presented to him, represents the state on official occasions, and gives continuity to the government during periods when there may not be a cabinet functioning. And he may be asked to exercise emergency powers as chief of state in a crisis.

Ordinarily, the Governor-General, like the sovereign he represents, is "above politics." But his influence may be great, or little, depending upon his personality and background. In Mr. Jinnah's case, "influence" is hardly the word. As Governor-General, president of the Constituent Assembly, president of the Moslem League, the ruling political party, and acknowledged "father of his country," the Qaid-i-Azam, or Great Leader, Jinnah was the next thing to a dictator.

This tall, spare, brilliant and cynical man received the British abdication in a curiously subdued ceremony on the steps of Karachi's Constituent Assembly Building on a sultry August 14. Since Mountbatten had to perform the same function at Parliament House in New Delhi on the stroke of midnight that night—the Indians wanted not a second's delay in the transfer of power—Pakistan was the first-born of the twin Dominions.

One occasionally reads that the moment for the hand-over in New Delhi was selected by astrologers as the most propitious time by the signs of the planets. This couldn't be more wrong, as the British say. In fact, according to the astrologers, the time chosen was most unfortunate, and there were forebodings of evil omens for the newborn state.

Nevertheless, there must have been a million Indians in the square outside the round, red sandstone Parliament building when Jawaharlal Nehru emerged as the first Prime Minister of a free India. Mountbatten was also cheered—there was a joke that the Indians were changing Mountbatten to "Mount-bannerji"—and British prestige in India was never so high as at the moment she relinquished her long rule over the country. It was a mad, joyous scene that night, and it was repeated the following day at the official raising of the Indian flag, when even Mountbatten and Nehru had difficulty getting through the singing, laughing crowd to their places at the flagstaff.

The one man, above all others, who should have been present on this supreme occasion, the man who had done most to win India's freedom, was not there. Characteristically, Mohandas K. Gandhi, the "architect of Indian independence," chose to stay quietly in Calcutta, away from what should have been his triumph.

India's joy was soon drowned in blood.

The rivalries and inequities that led to partition still existed on both sides of the artificial boundary between India and Pakistan, a line then not completely delineated or manned by border guards and customs posts. Because of the widespread mingling of communities, it had not been possible to divide territories so that all Hindus were on one side, all Moslems on the other, without making the map of the subcontinent an impossible crazy quilt of administrative enclaves. Division on the basis of majority provinces left more than fifteen million Hindus and Sikhs in Pakistan, and nearly fifty million Moslems in India. The fact of partition dramatized the wrongs, both real and fancied, that each had suffered at the hands of the other. Immediately after August 15, bitterness welled over, and blood began to flow in unparalleled carnage.

There had been countless communal riots in India's past history, and some of the worst had grown out of the Moslem agitation for Pakistan. But by August of 1947, with Moslem demands satisfied, religious disturbances had virtually ceased. Then, with division of the Punjab, the powerful and mili-

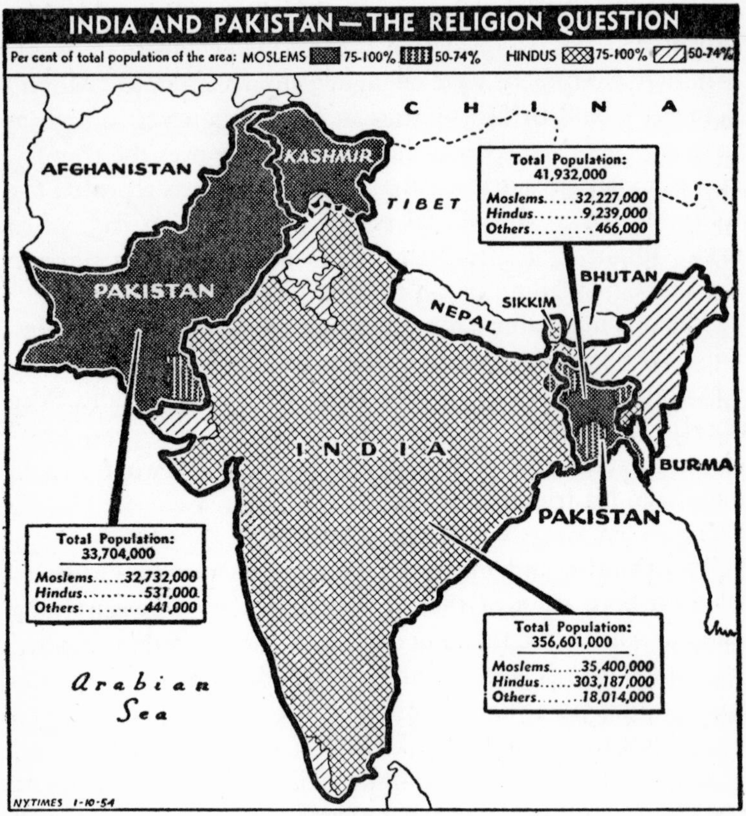

tant Sikh community became the center of a new chain reaction that quickly engulfed most of North India and Pakistan.

It is an academic question now where the trouble started and who attacked first. A known fact is that the Sikhs had been stirred up by their leaders, and that the killing began in their domain in the Punjab. Most of the six million Sikhs in the world were prosperous farmers in this rich province, which was the grain bowl of undivided India. The partition line cut through the Sikh lands, leaving the more desirable areas in Moslem Pakistan. It is argued by Pakistanis that if the Sikh leaders had immediately pledged their political allegiance to Karachi, no conflict would have occurred and

that they are considered part of the Hindu society for legislative purposes.

Today, so many young Sikhs are cutting their hair and shaving their beards, thus becoming indistinguishable from other Indians, that at least one authority believes the Sikh community will lose its separate identity within the century.

Somewhere in their martial past, all Sikhs added the word Singh, meaning lion, to their names. It is not strictly correct, however, to use Singh as if it were a surname; it should be coupled with the preceding family or given name. Thus, one would not properly say "Mr. Singh" in addressing a Sikh, but "Mr. Mohan Singh," "Mr. Sobha Singh," and so forth. In numerous cases the Singh is followed by a caste or clan name, as in the case of the proprietor of the Hotel Imperial in New Delhi, Rai Bahadur Mohan Singh Oberoi. Disregarding for convenience the Rai Bahadur, which is a title, one would call him "Mr. Oberoi." But while all Sikhs are Singhs, not all Singhs are Sikhs. The "lion" occurs also in the names of Rajputs, Jats, and others.

Sikh nationalism, excited by such fiery leaders as the venerable Master Tara Singh, was a factor in the Punjab outbreak, and still plays a not insignificant part in Indian politics today. The great Sikh kingdom consolidated by Maharajah Ranjit Singh, with its capital at Lahore, extended far into what is now Pakistan, and was one of the last powerful native states to fall to the British in 1849. Several small Sikh princely states survived in the Punjab until the consolidation under the Nehru government. The most powerful of these was Patiala, whose stately maharajah, a magnificent figure of an Indian prince standing six feet six, is the leading personality of his community today.

Whether or not the Punjab massacre originated in the Sikh princely states, as was widely said at the time, these tiny principalities quickly became the arsenal of embattled Sikhs determined to hurl the last Moslem out of East Punjab. The *kirpan* was unsheathed against the ancient enemy, and the

Sikh war cry, *Sat Sri Akul!* (God is truth), rang over the parched Punjab plains while Moslems rose to their own dreaded battle summons, *Allah-o-Akbar, ya Allah!*

In retaliation and counterretaliation, the Punjabi Moslems, renowned warriors themselves, threw themselves against the West Punjab Sikhs with gun, sword and lance, while the East Punjab Sikhs, soon joined by fanatical Hindus led by the RSS, fell upon Moslems in Delhi, Bihar and the United Provinces (now Uttar Pradesh).

Delhi, the capital of the Moguls, was at least half a Moslem city. When word reached the capital of what was going on in the Punjab, Hindus and Sikhs surged into the *mohallas*, or Moslem quarters, inflicting indiscriminate death and destruction. Naturally New Delhi, the adjacent modern capital city, was not spared. Since most servants in New Delhi were Moslems, murderous bands at once began the rounds of the servants' quarters of the upper- and middle-class bungalows in the residential sections.

The United States Embassy hostel, The *Taj*, a wartime senior officers' billet across the street from the Hotel Imperial, was under armed guard. I took my bearer, Khalil Khan, over there to join the protected servants of the Embassy people, who were all friends of mine. (In those days we were a small American community in New Delhi, and it was possible to know everybody.) Eventually Khalil Khan and the others were transferred to the *Purana Qila*, or Old Fort, where thousands of frightened Moslems were gathered until they could be evacuated to Pakistan. The vast area inside the ancient walls, said to be the site of the legendary three-thousand-year-old city of Indraprastha—the forerunner of nine cities of Delhi—became an immense refugee camp policed and guarded by the British Army and ministered to by Delhi health authorities and compassionate residents, including many foreigners. Khalil Khan eventually got to Pakistan, and I last heard of him in his native Rawalpindi. Thousands of others were less fortunate.

The highway to the airport was a favorite place for Hindus and Sikhs to waylay groups of Moslems attempting to escape by air. Frantic Moslems jammed into the Delhi main railway station, hoping to get onto one of the fantastically crowded trains to Lahore, were also easy prey.

One day I had word that a terrific riot was going on at the railway station. I rushed over there—it was about five miles from the hotel—and found the platform running with blood. Inert forms lay on the tracks, and I counted more than fifty dead bodies being carted out of the station on baggage hand-trucks. At police stations, lorries pulled in with loads of dead, who were dumped unceremoniously onto the ground in heaps.

Corpses lay in the landscaped streets of New Delhi, bloating in the heat. Many of the Moslem quarters were a shambles. I watched the sickening spectacle of screaming crowds hurling huge stones, as heavy as they could lift, from rooftops into the flimsy Moslem shops, which often also were the dwelling places of the owners. Looting was rampant; men, women and children, of all ages, scuttled away from the scenes of carnage with kitchenware, clothing, furniture—as much as they could carry. Once I saw a policeman kneel on one knee, take deliberate aim with his rifle, and bring down a fleeing looter with a single magnificent shot. But mostly, in the early stages, the police were wholly in sympathy with the miscreants, and were inclined to look the other way if they didn't actually help the rioters.

As refugees from the Punjab poured into Delhi, their accounts of their own sufferings at the hands of Moslems enraged relatives and friends who ordinarily would have remained peaceful citizens. As the refugees moved to other cities, they took the hysteria with them. Hindus from Karachi jammed the coastal vessels to Bombay, and soon that city, which had been quiet, also gave in to communal frenzy. Hindu and Moslem families who had lived together without strife for generations were suddenly swept into the vortex of passions that quickly threatened the existence of Nehru's government.

Fortunately, the madness did not extend to the south in any serious degree. The historic region of conflict between Hindus and Moslems had been confined generally to the Indus basin and the Gangetic plain, while the south was spared the centuries-old build-up of passions that exploded climactically in the Punjab in 1947. South Indians, reading in their newspapers what was happening in the north, wondered if their countrymen had been stricken suddenly with mass homicidal insanity. It was true, as apologists for India pointed out at the time, that most of the country was peaceful; but that fact did not lessen the enormity of the terror that swept the North.

The Indian Army command, which was still British, rushed Gurkha troops to the Delhi area. These tough Nepalese hillmen, and some other units brought in from the south, were unaffected by communalism. (The army of pre-partition India had already been divided between the two new Dominions, Moslem units being assigned to Pakistan. There were many Moslem officers in non-Moslem units who chose to stay with India, but the basis of the division of armed forces was religious.) The Indian press information officials were extremely touchy on the subject of the Army's conduct during the riots; numerous foreign correspondents were hauled on the carpet for mentioning, in their dispatches, the heroic part that the British and the Gurkhas played in restoring order. Officials invariably demanded to know "why correspondents didn't give the Indians credit."

It was not well known at the time that the Nehru government itself was shaky. Nehru was extremely put out with the foreign correspondents, whom he accused of exaggerating the carnage. The implication was that the foreign newsmen, generally speaking, were sensationalists at best, and interested in showing that the Indians were not capable of governing themselves. Looking back, I think the fault of the correspondents, myself included, was in failing to impart in their daily dispatches a sense of the full enormity of what was going on around us. Years afterward, I heard Nehru refer to the 1947 massacres in terms much stronger than correspondents generally used at the time.

Some old-line British types may have been secretly gleeful at the debacle that so swiftly overtook India upon the departure of the foreign rulers. Many felt sorry for Nehru and the others who devoted their lives to the cause of India's independence; they didn't deserve to have this happen to them.

One of Nehru's broadcasts, in which he spoke angrily of the foreign correspondents "abusing India's hospitality," nearly got a group of us mobbed in a café in Lahore one evening.

We had been touring the principal trouble areas, and were relaxing after dinner in Stiffle's night club. A group of blazing-eyed young men surrounded our table and accused us—using Nehru's own words—of "abusing India's hospitality." We were in a really dangerous situation for a few minutes. It occurred to us only later that we were in Pakistan, not India; apparently these young Lahore Moslems still thought of themselves as Indians in those days. The incident sticks in my mind as an impressive demonstration of Nehru's power to mobilize opinion with a phrase.

Nehru was personally courageous in his efforts to allay the mob spirit that had taken possession of the Punjab. With the late Liaquat Ali Khan, the first Prime Minister of Pakistan, he toured the worst areas, and let his famous temper loose on sullen crowds of Sikhs and Hindus on the scenes of some of the most conspicuous outrages. It is not beyond imagination that he took his life in his hands on more than one occasion as he sailed into the midst of a murderous mob.

Ronnie Stead of the *Christian Science Monitor*, Bob Miller of United Press, and I took a refugee train from Delhi to Lahore. The train was incredibly jammed with about three thousand Moslem refugees bound for Pakistan, carrying what small possessions they could stuff into portable bundles. They rode the rods, hung onto the sides of the cars, and lay on the roofs. They would have bulged out the windows had these not been covered with heavy wire netting for security as the train passed through the most dangerous areas of the eastern Punjab. We three had obtained a first-class compartment by a generous distribution of tips at the teeming Delhi station, and we steadfastly ignored the furious assaults on our locked doors at every station where the train stopped throughout the night.

Refugee trains were regularly attacked by Sikh bands, with indescribable slaughter of the Moslem passengers. The same thing was happening to Hindu and Sikh refugees in Pakistan.

An American businessman described an incident on a train he was riding from Peshawar to Lahore. A group of Moslems halted the train in the countryside, and demanded that all Sikhs get off. When no one made a move, the Moslems stated, in a polite and matter-of-fact tone, that if the Sikhs did not disembark voluntarily, there would be no alternative but to haul them out through the windows. This, they pointed out, would put everybody concerned to unnecessary trouble and pain, and the end would indubitably be the same. The Sikhs appreciated the reasoning. Thirteen Sikhs then stepped quietly from the cars, and stood unresisting while the Moslems methodically brained them with hockey sticks. They were luckier than the Moslem gentleman whom a Sikh band cut to pieces on our train, in the compartment next door.

Ronnie and Bob and I wanted to see firsthand what happened to these refugee trains. We chose the Frontier Mail, leaving Delhi at night.

It was about seven o'clock in the morning when I was awakened by Bob Miller's shout, "Here come the boys!"

4

"Very Wicked, Indeed!"

NOW I HAVE AN IDEA HOW THE EARLY SETTLERS IN THE WEST must have felt when their covered-wagon trains were attacked on the trail by red Indians. Except that our train was mechanized, we were in much the same situation. We had stopped in the middle of an arid plain, an endless vista of yellow earth dotted with small, sick-looking shrubs that stretched away as far as one could see until the landscape blended with the dun-colored haze of dust.

The train was encircled by a whooping, screaming band of half-naked brown men. Their black hair was bound into round topknots, but long, greasy-looking strands hung untidily about their bearded faces. Their teeth gleamed evilly as they grimaced and howled. More joined them from the concealment of the dust-covered shrubbery. All were waving swords, spears, axes and clubs about their unshorn heads.

I reflected that there is probably no more fearsome-looking human creature in the world than a Sikh on the warpath, especially in the early morning when he has left off his turban, which is put away for the night, and his wild hair streams in the hot wind.

There was a brief rattle of Sten-gun fire, but the advancing Sikhs paid no attention. It was our impression that the train's armed guard was deliberately firing into the air.

On the opposite side of the compartment from where I was looking, there was the sound of splintering wood. I turned in time to see a husky young Sikh tugging at the steel screen over the window with the hooked point of what appeared to be a medieval battle-ax. The screen gave little resistance to the grinning warrior's strength and leverage on the long ax handle. As the heavy wire net dropped to the ground, twanging, he poked the head of the ax through the double-glass window. The panes tinkled to the floor in bits.

We looked at the Sikh, wondering what to do. Hit him with a portable typewriter, maybe. This experience wasn't being fun.

But there was no need to worry about our own safety. The Sikh peered into the compartment, and as soon as he saw our white faces he laughed loudly, waved his hand in a friendly fashion, and turned away.

We were to find that in all this insane orgy of killing that was to continue in North India for weeks, no one had the slightest intention of harming a white man. We could go anywhere without fear. The blood-lust was directed solely and entirely at the other religious community.

Indians, too, were safe if they could prove that they were not of the group being attacked. This was not often a problem. No one, of course, could mistake a Sikh, but Hindus and Moslems, though belonging generally to the same race, seemed to have distinguishing marks and characteristics that set them apart at once, things that would not appear to a foreigner new in the country. For example, as I learned later, a man with a tattoo on his arm—perhaps his initials—would be a Hindu, for Moslems do not take to this custom. The cut of a beard might be a giveaway. And in many instances, no doubt, an infusion of Afghan or Persian blood would give a Moslem a distinctive cast of feature immediately recognizable to a Hindu. A Moslem mistakenly caught by his fellow religionists could always prove his identity, of course, by showing that he had been circumcised, and there was wholesale disrobing, forcible and otherwise, in many trains that were attacked.

Our train, we were to learn later, had been halted by a standard ruse of the attackers on both sides. One of the conspirators—in this instance, undoubtedly a Sikh—would get on the train at some station with orders to pull the emergency air-brake cord at an agreed point along the line. As the train shuddered to a halt, the marauders struck, and the engine driver was not permitted to proceed until they had satisfied themselves that every member of the opposed community, man, woman and child, had been killed. As a side activity the attackers might do a bit of looting, and any passably attractive female was likely to be taken away.

After a period of bedlam, of shouts and screams punctuated by an occasional burst from the Sten gun, the raiders faded away and the train shivered into motion. When we pulled into the next station, which was Bhatinda, we got out to survey the damage. The door to the compartment next to ours was open, and blood was trickling from the floor onto the steps outside. We looked in, and saw a man lying on the floor. He was a respectable-looking, well-dressed Moslem, in his middle thirties. He lay twitching, and covered with blood. There were cuts all over his head and body, and one thumb dangled from a thread of skin. The station was full of people, but no one but us was paying any attention to this man.

We called the conductor, then the station master, but it was at least an hour before a Sikh doctor appeared to attend to the man, whose occasional spasmodic movements showed that he was still alive. The Sikh doctor looked at him and went away. After another long wait, several men brought a stretcher and took the man away in leisurely, careless fashion. We never found out who he was, or if he lived or died. He didn't look like he had much chance.

The way he was being handled reminded me of another grisly incident I had witnessed a few days before, on the big bridge across the Jumna River in Delhi. A crowd was milling about at one end of the bridge, where I was, and police were standing by in their usual idle fashion in the early stages of the Delhi riots, before authority got a firm hand. The mob parted and then, with police assisting to clear a lane, four men appeared carrying another man by his hands and feet. He was streaming blood. While police pushed and shoved to give them more room, they advanced a few yards onto the bridge, then tossed their human burden over the rail and into the river, like a sack of grain. He was taken away by the swirling water, and that was that—no one paid any further attention. Was the man thrown in the river alive or dead? No one in the mob, including the police, seemed to know or care.

While we were waiting at the Bhatinda station, we met two fellow passengers, a seamy, spare man and a weather-beaten woman, who turned out to be a British missionary couple with long experience in India. The woman, wagging an angry finger, had transfixed a well-dressed, ferret-faced Sikh whose oiled beard was curled over a thread that ran under his chin from ear to ear, in a fashion common among Sikhs who like to keep their whiskers neat and out of the way.

The woman was convinced that this Sikh was the conspirator who had pulled the cord to stop the train. Her clipped British accent implied that while she was not shocked nor even surprised by this unspeakable crime, she considered it very bad behavior, which should not go unreproved. The Sikh squirmed and grinned sheepishly, like a schoolboy caught in some flagrant naughtiness. And this was just the way the firm British matron was treating him. She shook her finger under his aquiline nose and concluded sternly, "That was very wicked of you! Very wicked, indeed!"

The murder on the train confirmed a conviction I had begun to form in Delhi, that the Indians are not skillful killers. The newspapers always described the victims of such affrays as having been "stabbed," and until I began to see such victims myself I automatically thought of a stabbing as being a clean knife-thrust, neat and conclusive. But from observation I found that in India to be "stabbed" may mean being cut to ribbons, butchered alive. As I became accustomed to violent death, I could regard murder with detachment, but I never ceased to be revolted by the Indians' botchy technique.

Indians were efficient enough, though, when they merely meant to maim. Prowling through the refugee hospitals and camps, I observed that they cut off hands and women's breasts with surgical neatness. The only conclusion I can reach from this is suggested by the fact that cutting off members as punishment has some tradition behind it.

There should be no misapprehension, from this account, that the crimes of the Moslems were less than those of the Hindus and Sikhs. In my observation on both sides of the India-Pakistan border, one was as bad as the other.

The rutted roads of the Punjab were choked with bullock-cart caravans, plodding their slow way in both directions, until well after the terrible summer heat had passed, and the nights became near freezing. Some of these convoys, under Indian and Pakistani army guard on their respective territories, were more than sixty miles long. The clouds of dust they raised could be seen from airplanes long before the crawling caravans themselves were in sight. While they were in unfriendly territory the creeping wagon trains, making at the most four miles an hour, were always subject to sudden raids, with stragglers at the nether end being cut off and slain, and their women taken captive.

Abduction of women was one of the sorest points on both sides. When an uneasy peace finally settled on the Punjab after vast populations had been exchanged, both sides put reclamation teams to work to try to recover kidnaped wives and daughters. This humanitarian labor uncovered many human tragedies in the following years. There were women who didn't want to be returned to their homes because they were afraid, with much justification, that they would never again be socially acceptable to their own people. Others, as time passed, had children by their captors, and preferred to go on with their new lives. Some of these, through overzealousness on the part of well-meaning welfare workers, were more or less forcibly torn from their adopted homes and sent back to former environments that were now strange and unwelcome. But in other cases, social organizations conducted successful campaigns to find husbands for the willingly recovered single women, who presumably lived happily ever after.

Lists of rescued females are still published periodically by the press, in hopes they will be seen by relatives whose whereabouts are unknown. Meanwhile, many recriminations have been exchanged between the governments of India and Pakistan on the cases of abducted women, and it is doubtful if either country will ever be satisfied that it has fully recovered its own. This is but one of the many lasting bitternesses growing out of the partition upheavals.

Although the impetus to the Punjab disturbances sprang from economic dissatisfactions, the conflict, spread over thousands of square miles in hundreds of cities, towns and villages, quickly reverted to the ancient religious complexion of the Hindu-Moslem struggles of generations past.

Forcible conversions from one religion to the other took place on both sides. This phenomenon was especially affecting to the Hindus and Sikhs. A Moslem, forced to recite the Ramayana at the point of a sword, might oblige with mental reservations, and return to the Islamic fold as soon as he could make his escape—actually never having left it. But a Hindu, made to eat beef and worship in the mosque, would have forfeited his caste and put himself beyond the pale of his social order.

An old Sikh, whose son was shorn of his hair and beard and made to swear by the Koran, was inconsolable though the boy was recovered unharmed. "My son is no longer a

Sikh," he wailed. To his mind, nothing more could be done about the matter.

Millions who were not involved directly in the religious strife suffered immense economic dislocation and personal inconvenience. It happened that on both sides the religious minority included the bulk of certain essential classes. In India, many of the artisans, machinists and household servants were Moslems, while in Pakistan the white-collar professions were crippled by the loss of Hindus. The Karachi government went to great lengths to keep the Hindu Untouchables, who did the city's scavenging, from moving out, lest the accumulation of uncollected refuse lead to epidemics.

The scavenger problem bothered the Indian government, too. Caste Hindus could not do this work under any conditions, so the government chartered airplanes to fly squads of Untouchable "sweepers" to the crowded refugee encampments. When I visited the Moslem refugees jammed by thousands into Delhi's great seventeenth century mosque, the Jama Masjid, the filth was ankle-deep, and the one complaint of the inmates was that "the government hasn't sent us sweepers."

The millions of refugees who made up the pitiful wagon trains of those grim and bloody treks across the Punjab were able to take with them only such possessions as they could pile into carts or carry on their backs. Many a rich man in Delhi or Lahore arrived in his new homeland penniless and without a roof. Their bank accounts and securities were sequestered, their land and houses occupied by refugees from the other side. Ever since 1948, efforts have been made by the two governments to reach a settlement on the involuntary exchange of property, but divergent points of view on methods and values have impeded a mutually satisfactory agreement. The result has been an enduring bitterness, which many Indians and Pakistanis believe is a far greater hindrance to amicable relations than any of the other major disputes between New Delhi and Karachi.

According to the best estimates in round numbers, six million Moslems fled from India to Pakistan, while five million Hindus and Sikhs moved from Pakistan to India, in the great migration. The exchange has been a continual though diminishing process in the following years, so that today the figure on each side is higher by perhaps a million. There has also been a continual return of refugees to their old homes as conditions settled, but the numbers are insignificant in the over-all picture, and furthermore, they are hard to pin down, since there has always been a great two-way traffic of itinerant laborers, traders, and smugglers across the Indo-Pakistani frontiers.

Although the Hindus and Sikhs displaced from Pakistan were fewer in number than the Moslems driven out of India, the former were deprived of greater wealth, for they were the landowners, moneylenders and businessmen of their communities. The evacuation of Hindus and Sikhs from Lahore, for instance, deprived that great Punjab city of more than 80 per cent of its registered taxpayers, so a Pakistani official told me. According to Indian government estimates, property abandoned by Hindus and Sikhs in Pakistan came to about eight billion dollars, while the Moslems who fled India, being a poorer class on the whole, lost only about four hundred million dollars in movable and immovable wealth.

Pakistan, being in no position financially to entertain India's huge claim for compensation, has insisted that restitution be worked out on a private, individual basis. But India has held out for a government-to-government settlement. In the deadlock that has ensued, both governments have been devising their separate systems of compensation to their own refugees, which naturally can come nowhere near to settling claims satisfactorily, or allaying individual bitterness.

As I traveled frequently between India and Pakistan as a

correspondent, I was often asked by persons on both sides to "take a look at my old home"—homes they never expected to see again. The request was accompanied by a wistfulness often near to tears. The same emotion attended countless importunities to look up this or that dear relative or old friend on the other side. This even happened when I moved from the Indian to the Pakistani front, or vice versa, during the war in Kashmir: officers on one side or the other would ask me to "give my love" to a captain or colonel who had been a lifelong comrade in arms but was now a nominal enemy.

These friendships and cherished associations endure with the older folk, and both India and Pakistan are full of homesick people. But this reservoir of good will, which should promote the closest ties of friendship between the two countries, is fast being drained, and a new generation is growing up with only suspicion and resentment of the brother nation.

In many cities of India and Pakistan, streets are still lined with the miserable huts of the displaced persons who have been unable to adjust, or find a place in communities that were already shockingly overcrowded before they came. These thousands of noisome hovels, and the sight of people sleeping on the sidewalks and under bridges for lack of any shelter at all, tend to obscure the fact that both India and Pakistan have done a magnificent job of resettling and rehabilitating the vast majority of the refugees, who have been successfully absorbed. Few countries could have accomplished so much against such enormous odds, at a time when the outlook for a new government was far from bright without added burdens of a cataclysmic social upheaval.

The refugee element is an inflammable and highly vocal political force in both India and Pakistan. It is they, principally, who keep alive the communal animosities that were supposed to disappear when the Moslems were given a separate state. Personal suffering and loss of homes and happiness by one community at the hands of another cannot be forgotten in the lifetime of the victims, and probably of their children. These understandable resentments continue to be a festering sore in relations between India and Pakistan, however much the leaders of the two countries may strive for amity.

And, as a natural corollary, bitter memories perpetuate distrust between the two principal religious groupings in both countries. The ten million Hindus remaining in Pakistan, mostly in East Bengal, continue to feel uneasy, with good reason.

India's forty million Moslems, though their lot in general is no doubt better under a secular government than that of the Pakistani Hindus in a frankly Islamic state, are given cause to suspect the real sentiments of the Hindu majority. Despite the guarantees in the law, a member of the minority in either country is likely to encounter furtive, perhaps often unconscious, discrimination in his dealings with officials who belong to the majority. If a Moslem in India loses a court case or is passed over in an examination for a government job, he is likely to believe that he has received unfair treatment because he is a Moslem. This will be quite true often enough to give point to the minority's uneasiness. The same thing happens to Hindus in Pakistan.

Members of the minority crossing the border from one country to the other undergo extraordinary harassment by customs and immigration officials on both sides, for such persons are peculiarly subject to suspicion, not without cause, of being spies or smugglers. Then there are organizations like the All-India Hindu Mahasabha (Great Society) that agitate a policy of "Hindus first," and are in the forefront of all anti-Pakistani and anti-Moslem propaganda.

The death of Mahatma Gandhi at the hands of a Hindu fanatic removed the most potent individual force for tolerance, not only in India but also in Pakistan.

Gandhi's last fast was undertaken to bring an end to religious conflicts in Delhi. After a few days, leading members of the Hindu, Sikh and Moslem communities in the capital city came to his side and signed a pledge of peace. The Mahatma (Great Spirit) also singlehandedly brought peace to Calcutta, until that time the stormiest city in India. In Calcutta he was joined in his fast by the Pakistani Moslem political leader, Hussain Shaheed Suhrawardy, who is about as Gandhian a personality as the Aga Khan.

Gandhi restrained militant Hindu protagonists in the Indian government, like the late Deputy Prime Minister and political boss Sardar Vallabhbhai Patel, from vindictive measures against Pakistan at the time of greatest strain between the two new governments. It was for his solicitude and generosity toward Moslems that Gandhi was assassinated, and his death was mourned as sincerely in Karachi and Lahore as in New Delhi, for with his passing the Moslems lost their greatest and most powerful friend.

After the disturbances in the Punjab and surrounding territories were brought under control, there was no major outbreak of religious conflict until the Hindus and Moslems of Calcutta and East Bengal rose against each other in the winter of 1949-1950. This episode cost India dearly among the predominantly Moslem inhabitants of the disputed state of Jammu and Kashmir.

The latest Bengal strife came to an end when Nehru and Liaquat Ali Khan met in New Delhi in April, 1950, and drew up the so-called "Charter for Minorities" guaranteeing equal rights and protection. But prejudice and hate cannot be decreed or legislated out of existence. One has the feeling, even when all is calm, that hostility and suspicion still simmer beneath the surface.

It is possible, one hopes, that settlement of the evacuee property question, the Kashmir issue, distribution of canal waters, and other disputes between India and Pakistan will eventually damp these smoldering fires.

5

Happy Birthday, Maharajah!

All buildings in Delhi are constructed with immensely thick masonry walls, to keep out the heat. But in winter they keep the cold in, and it is like living in a damp cavern. Though later I was to consider the Delhi winter delightful, in 1947 I had come out of fourteen consecutive years in the tropics with hardly a break—all my visits to the States since 1935 had been timed for summer—so when the temperature dipped to the low forties at night I thought I was freezing to death. Therefore, I was delighted to accept an invitation to be the guest of the Nizam of Hyderabad over Christmas. The Nizam's dominions lie well below the Tropic of Cancer, and it is never cold there.

This was to be the first of many visits to Indian princely states. I had met a few maharajahs—Bharatpur, Patiala, Sirmur and the Yuvaraj of Cutch—in New Delhi. Bharatpur, I think, was the first. I asked him a frivolous question, "How does it feel to be a maharajah?" "It's bloody awful," he replied. "Everybody fawns around, and you don't know whether people are your friends or whether they just want something. That's why I like Americans; they treat me as an ordinary fellow, and call me by my nickname." His nickname was "Indu," and he was almost a god to twenty million Jats, a Hindu caste of North India.

His Exalted Highness Mir Sir Osman Ali Khan, the Nizam of Hyderabad, was the premier ruling prince of India and reputedly the richest man in the world. Though I was his guest for a week, I was not able to meet him, for he had refused to see any journalist since an American correspondent had published some of the many legends about the Nizam's idiosyncrasies in a popular weekly magazine, some years before. I only saw him pass by in his car, an old English Humber. It was not until years later, in New Delhi, when he had been deprived of his power and much of his wealth, that I was able to speak to him. And I found him an unassuming, gracious man.

Then over sixty, the Nizam had approximately one concubine for every year of his age, and irreverent wags sometimes referred to him as "His Exhausted Highness." But he became a father with great regularity, the last time (that I know of) after he was sixty-five.

The Nizam, although his negotiable wealth in jewels, precious metals and hoarded bank notes alone was reputed to approximate two billion dollars, was a renowned miser. It was said that he personally supervised his concubines' kitchen, to see to it that no rice was wasted, and that the maintenance of each of his odalisques cost no more than eight annas, or ten cents, a day. I couldn't help reflecting that I had to pay out three times that much to keep a Scotty dog in the Hotel Imperial.

When you had tea with the Nizam, I was told, you got exactly one cup, with sugar and milk already in it, and one British cigarette—no more. (The ruler himself smoked cheap Hyderabad *bidis.*) He skimped atrociously on his personal laundry, to prolong the life of his clothes. When he gave a dinner for the nobles of his domain—the Nizam was empowered to confer the coveted title of Nawab on favored subjects—the guests were not only expected to bring gifts of cash, but were informed beforehand exactly how much. When His Exalted Highness was entertained—by order—in the house of a subject noble, he was sometimes known to order the valuable tableware and plates moved to his palace, if he took a fancy to them.

There is no exact estimate of the Nizam's wealth in jewels, and it is generally conceded that the question is academic anyway, for it is accepted that if he were to place them on the market all at once, the value of the world's diamond stocks would be shattered. I was told that truckloads of solid gold bars lay somewhere in the palace gardens, overgrown with grass; I know only that once a slight disposal of this precious metal from the Nizam's hoard dropped the Bombay gold market ten points. And I had it on good authority that a great fortune in currency was found molding and disintegrating in burlap bags in the potentate's treasury.

From what I heard of the Nizam's collection of pearls, I once calculated that he had enough of these gems to pave Broadway from Times Square to Columbus Circle.

Once, according to a favorite story in India, the Nizam hired a European expert to appraise his pearls. After several weeks without word from the appraiser, the Nizam sent for him. "How long will it take you to finish the job?" he asked with some impatience. "Two or three years, Your Exalted Highness," the expert replied. "Good Lord," exclaimed the Nizam, "I couldn't possibly afford to pay you for all that time." And he was sacked forthwith.

I cannot vouch for these stories, which are frequently told in India, but I can add one of my own to the fund of anecdotes about the Nizam's fabulous wealth. In Hyderabad, I heard that the ruler kept an uncut diamond, as big as his fist, on his desk as a paperweight. I asked one of his secretaries if this was true.

"Good heavens no, what utter rot!" the secretary replied. "It's only an emerald!"

There was nothing niggardly about the Nizam's hospitality, though he did not appear personally in it. When he left his capital city, which was seldom, he used a private railway car with plumbing fixtures of solid gold. His only trip out of his state in my time in India was a journey to New Delhi, where he kept, but had almost never used, the most magnificent palace in the great concourse of princely residences around what is known as Princes' Park. (Most of these have been requisitioned by the Indian government; the Nizam's palace is now the number one guest house for official visitors.) In coming to New Delhi the Nizam decided to try his first airplane ride. For himself and a small retinue he chartered a Constellation, and made a trial run in it over Hyderabad city before trusting himself to the longer journey.

The Nizam's coffers bulged with the plunder of centuries, for his domain took in the legendary treasure vaults of Golconda, now an abandoned fortress city and a "must" for all tourists, just outside the city of Hyderabad.

But the inexhaustible source of the Nizam's fabulous yearly income was his revenue from private land holdings totaling seven thousand square miles—equal to the combined area of the states of Maryland and Delaware. When these and other possessions were eventually nationalized, the Indian government did not think it extravagant or out of line to grant the aging Nizam a privy purse, or pension, of two million dollars a year in return.

The Nizam was absolute ruler of a state about the size of Minnesota, with a population of eighteen million. Claiming direct descent from the Caliph Abu Bakr, successor to Mohammed, and allied to the family of the last Caliph of Islam through the marriage of two sons into the Turkish royal house, the Nizam is a figure in the Moslem world.

For siding consistently with the British in numerous Indian wars, the head of Hyderabad's ruling dynasty has enjoyed special favors, such as exclusive use of the honorific, "His Exalted Highness." The British Crown officially conferred upon the present Nizam the title, "Faithful Ally of the British Government," for rallying India's Moslems to the British cause in World War I. In World War II the Nizam, out of his great wealth, bought bombers for the Royal Air Force. His own state forces, with twenty-five thousand men and tanks, commanded by an Arab major general, was the most powerful princely army in India.

But neither his wealth nor his army saved the Nizam from the fate of the other Indian rulers, whose continued existence as autocrats stood in the way of the new India's relentless democratic progress.

The Maharajah of Bharatpur, "Indu," felt like apologizing because his shooting party, about two dozen of us, only got 359 ducks that day. "I usually shoot that many myself," he said. The record for the annual Bharatpur shoot, for about thirty guns, was 4,273.

The Bharatpur shoot was famous in Anglo-Indian sporting circles. A few miles from the city of Bharatpur, capital of the state, every year the rains filled a broad, shallow depression, forming a lake. Millions of ducks headed annually for this sanctuary, coming from as far as Russia and Siberia, as had been proved by banding the migratory birds. Every winter His Highness invited guests for a special week end of sport, allotting them to the best "butts" according to rank. Each shooter had a gunbearer, and a man to dash into the water to retrieve the game that was shot down. The butts were furnished with beer and sandwiches, and there were vehicles to deliver the sportsmen back to the palace. The shooting was always followed by an informal dinner, at which the beautiful Maharani would appear.

Ordinarily, the birds came over the lake in clouds, and any kind of a shot could bring them down like rain, as fast as one could work the triggers of a double-barreled shotgun. On this occasion the birds were not rising as plentifully as usual, so Indu was disconsolate. For diversion, after dinner, he had a servant bring the palace's pet cheetah into the drawing room.

The great cat, as big as a Great Dane and spotted like a

leopard, had been brought from Kenya and was meant for hunting deer, but Indu had never let him taste blood, as he wished to keep the animal as a household pet. His purr sounded like the drone of an approaching B-29, and when he licked pats of butter from our fingers his rough tongue nearly took off the skin.

We all thought the cheetah was very cute. He would rub his enormous head against your knee like a kitten, and would roll over to have his stomach scratched.

"What's his name?" I asked.

"Well, since he's the only cheetah around here, we just call him Cheetah," Indu said. "He doesn't need any other name for identification."

Indu, still in his thirties, was the reigning head of what had been a great ruling house. At one time Bharatpur, which is about one hundred miles due south of Delhi, had been a powerful state. One of Indu's ancestors had captured Delhi and brought the great gates of the city to Bharatpur, where they may be seen today. Now they are the gates of Bharatpur city.

On the occasion of that conquest, Indu related, bullock carts loaded with loot formed a solid train all the way from Delhi to Bharatpur. The ancestor also sacked Agra, and was seriously considering moving the Taj Mahal to Bharatpur, stone by stone. He was stabbed to death by a Moslem on the steps of the famous monument.

To this day, the Bharatpur ruling family has little affection for Moslems. The state was the scene of bloody massacres during the partition disturbances of 1947, when it was estimated that one hundred thousand Moslems were driven out. Indu's younger brother, Raja Girraj Saran Singhji—better known as "Bachu," and a popular member of the younger princely set—avers that this is a slander on Bharatpur, that the number was not more than half that.

Bachu, who was to become one of my closest Indian friends, was exiled to London by the Indian government until the riots were well over, as it was thought in New Delhi that this Jat prince's presence in Bharatpur was hardly calculated to enhance communal harmony. Several years later Bachu had the satisfaction of defeating a deputy minister of the Nehru government in the first national elections, and he now is an active Member of Parliament representing Bharatpur. He is a member of no political party, and he doesn't have to be to get elected in Bharatpur, where Bachu's family has an unassailable religious position, next to divine.

As the religious leader of twenty million Jats—Bachu's figure—the Maharajah of Bharatpur was a powerful personage, holding a position of high respect among his brother princes, although the state in course of time had shrunk to an area of less than two thousand square miles, with a population of about half a million.

When the government of India merged Bharatpur into a union of small neighboring states, thus destroying the identity of a proud kingdom (and simultaneously stripping Indu of his sovereign powers), New Delhi was apprehensive of trouble at the official ceremony for the change-over. Troops were posted in the capital city in case the resentful Jats made a demonstration. Nothing of note happened, but the older folk, particularly, of Bharatpur felt it was a day of shame for a people whose ancestors had held off the British legions until treachery from within opened the gates of the impregnable fort.

Indu took his loss hard. He sought solace in religion, and for some time spent his days making *puja* (prayers) to the gods. The young Maharajah ruined his health by making a spectacular pilgrimage, measuring his length—lying prone, rising and stretching out flat again—around a sacred hill. It took him weeks, in the terrible month of July. Every evening, after he had prostrated, risen, and prostrated again for several miles, the Maharajah would be picked up by his Rolls-Royce limousine and be driven back to the palace for the night. The following morning, the Rolls would deposit him where he had left off.

The peasantry, who came for miles in great crowds to watch their former ruler's agonizing devotion, considered his act a saintly inspiration to piety, and he was extolled as a great holy man.

The belief in divinity, or near-divinity, of numerous Indian rulers was encouraged, I understand, by the ruling families themselves long ago, to strengthen their hold upon their subjects. The Maharajadhiraj (Great Prince of Princes) of Nepal is worshiped as a reincarnation of the god Vishnu, the "Preserver" in the Hindu trinity. (Nepal being an independent country, the monarch is now generally referred to as King.)

Visiting the Maharajah of Banaras, who has a fantastic collection of odd clocks from all over the world, I found his courtyard full of a constant stream of pilgrims who believe that he is the vicar of Lord Shiva (the "Destroyer" in the trinity) on earth.

In Travancore, the Maharajah is considered the earthly representative of Padmanabha, an aspect of Vishnu. The Maharajah administers the state on behalf of the god, who owns it. When Travancore was absorbed into the Indian Union, a special instrument of accession had to be drawn up under which the ruler transferred his powers with careful attention to preserving the status of Lord Padmanabha. In older times, the association with the god assured the position of the royal family above the people.

The Travancore rulers, who inherit through the female line in accordance with Hindu custom in that part of the country, incidentally were among the most enlightened in India. Literacy there is the highest, about 60 per cent; a legislative council was established to advise the ruler as far back as 1888, and women have had equal voting rights with men since 1933. Travancore was one of a number of princely states that, under wise rulers, were far more progressive than the British-governed provinces or, one might even say, India as a whole under the Congress government today.

The religious position of the princes in their former states has not been affected noticeably, at least among the older generation, by the loss of their ruling powers. They still preside over festivals and receive homage. Note was taken of their expensive religious obligations when the Indian government fixed privy purses.

For example, the Maharajah of Mysore (who is, incidentally, one of the world's leading patrons of fine music) is responsible for the glittering Dusserah festival in his state, one of the most magnificent pageants to be seen in India. For this event the palace is outlined in electric lights, and brilliant phalanxes of beautifully painted and caparisoned elephants march in the procession. The Maharajah of Mysore's elephant stables are world famous. It was here that Sabu, "elephant boy" of Hollywood fame, was discovered.

The state of Mysore is also renowned in India for its annual wild elephant roundup, called *kheddah*, and the staged elephant fights. The fighting elephants are made bellicose by feeding them buckets of grape brandy. The idea is to get them "fighting drunk," but on occasion an elephantine gladiator has reacted the opposite way, becoming maudlinly friendly on the immense draughts of strong liquor, and refusing to respond belligerently to any kind of provocation by his furious adversary.

The immense Maharajah of Manipur is a godly reincarnation who every year must re-enact a water battle with a demon. In mythology, the god whom the Maharajah represents won a victory—good always wins over evil in Hindu traditions—so His Highness can do no less. The fight is on the wide palace moat, with two long, slim boats engaged. Each is propelled by two dozen rowers. His Highness, dressed in rich green with an enormous headdress of peacock feathers and gold, sits in the prow of one of them, representing the god. It is quite a feat for His Highness to get into the slender craft, for he is one of the fattest men in India.

Rajputana, the broad western desert area now incorporated into the state of Rajasthan (Land of Princes), is called the home of Indian chivalry. The Rajputs, who go in for fierce mustaches twisted upward at the ends, claim a martial tradition going back to the beginnings of time. Many of the princely families of Hindu India belong to the Rajput caste, as do the rulers of Nepal. The Rajputs are of the second caste classification, the *kshatriya,* warriors and rulers, and they are prouder than the Brahmins, the number one caste, whom *kshatriyas* once held in subjection, according to their legends.

Historians believe the Rajputs are descended from Central Asian invaders of the fifth and sixth centuries, but the princes claim direct descent from the sun and moon through deities who came to earth from those celestial bodies. In the Rajputana states one hears reference to "solar and lunar dynasties," and one is assured that the Rajput ruling families are the most ancient royal houses on earth.

Of all the Rajputs, the Maharana of Udaipur (also called Mewar) is accepted without question as the bluest-blooded. His standard shows the blazing sun, whose direct descendant he is by tradition. When the Rajputana states were merged into the state of Rajasthan, the government of India wanted the Maharajah of Jaipur as the Rajpramukh (chief prince), or titular governor. So it was done, but the Rajputs could not accept anyone above the ruler of Udaipur, so New Delhi manufactured for the Maharana the unique title of Maharajpramukh (great chief prince), so that he nominally outranks the Rajpramukh, though he has no government functions.

The Maharajah of Jaipur, Rajpramukh of Rajasthan, is one of the Indian princes in the European "international set" and New York "café society." He is still, in his late thirties or early forties, one of the world's greatest polo players. Many of the princes excel at this sport, which is said to have originated in the state of Manipur, though Iran and many other places also claim to have been the birthplace of the game.

Fabulous treasures of the House of Jaipur are said to be stored in an ancient fortress, called the "Tiger Fort," on top of a brown hill behind the capital city. The hoard is guarded by members of a special caste who do nothing else, and each Maharajah of Jaipur is allowed, only once in his life and at a time of need, to go into the cache and select three objects. The present Maharajah has not yet availed himself of the privilege.

The ruler of Jaipur possesses a unique honor that is supposed to place him above all other mortals. The story goes that an ancestor, in the service of the Emperor Akbar, once captured four Afghan princes singlehanded. The pleased Emperor exclaimed to the noble Rajput warrior, "You are not a man, you are a man and a quarter!" And to this day, over his palaces in the coral-pink city of Jaipur, the Maharajah flies two flags, one above the other, the topmost one being a quarter the size of the first. And his name contains the title "Sawai," meaning "man and a quarter."

H.H. Jaipur is an enthusiastic amateur pilot. After a couple of crack-ups he was no longer able to pull on a riding boot, but that didn't stop him from continuing to play polo. Nowadays, in a scramble of flying horsemen, Jaipur's dashing figure can be distinguished as the one wearing cowboy "chaps" instead of boots, present of an American friend.

Many of the princes, like Jaipur, habitually wear the British Indian Army officer's uniform, with rows of decorations. One who earned his military rank on the battlefield, and not through the honorary route, is Lt. Col. His Highness the Maharao Raja of Bundi, one of the premier Rajput rulers. Young, handsome, the *beau ideal* of the Indian prince as pictured in romantic novels, His Highness of Bundi came out of World War II with the Military Cross, one of the highest British decorations for personal bravery under fire, won as a tank commander against the Japanese in Burma.

The high point of Bundi's year is the youthful prince's birthday *durbar*, or formal royal audience, in March. This spectacle, of a type still to be seen in the former princely states, takes place in an impressive old palace, now partly in ruins, where the Bundi family was reigning before Columbus discovered America. Enthroned in his ancestral *durbar* hall, the prince appears in rarely worn ceremonial dress, with strings of huge emeralds around his neck and wound about his striking Rajput turban. Noble retainers and humble villagers come forward one by one with token gifts—in the case of a peasant it may be a basket of flowers or vegetables—as a symbol of their fealty to the ancient dynasty, even though the ruling power no longer rests in the royal house.

Bundi's *durbar* is the occasion for a five-day house party, his one big blowout of the year, with guests including foreign ambassadors and other friends, who practically take over a first-class railway coach for the day-long journey from New Delhi. The state of Bundi in March being great tiger country, festivities include a shoot.

Not being a shooter, I watched this event from what amounted to a grandstand seat on a brown hillside across a dry gully where the tiger had his lair. The shooters themselves, in *machans* (tree platforms), had not nearly so good a view, for they could only see what went on in their own vicinity.

Tigers are easiest to find at the onset of the hot season, when streams dry up and the jungle beasts cannot prowl far from the known sources of water. The villagers, through their own intelligence system, are always well aware of the presence of a tiger in the neighborhood, for these animals are a menace to livestock and often to human life when they turn man-eater, which happens usually when the great cat is unable, because of wounds or old age, to run down his natural prey. His Highness' *shikaris* (professional hunters) located our tiger readily enough, and staked out a water buffalo to lure him to the vicinity of the *machans*. The tiger, as expected, gorged himself on the buffalo and retired to a cave to sleep off the feast.

In the morning we drove to the jungle in jeeps and took our assigned places, the shooters on the platforms, the rest of us facing them from the far side of the gulch. Then several hundred beaters—villagers and peasants who were as anxious to have the country rid of the tiger as the sportsmen were to shoot it—closed in around the cave with a deafening clamor of shouts to rouse the sleeping animal. From our grandstand seat we could see the whole show—the beaters converging on the cave in an open circle, and finally the tiger, irritated at being awakened, moving angrily through the dry scrub brush. The beaters were trying to drive him in the direction of the *machans*. Who got the first shot would depend upon which way the tiger decided to go. The beast ill-advisedly headed past the perch of His Highness, a deadly shot. A rifle cracked once, and His Highness had scored his sixty-seventh kill.

The party that night was in His Highness' private night club, where one of the cozy bars is carpeted, wall to wall, with a rug made of forty-five tiger skins, all H.H.'s personal trophies.

With India rapidly moving toward prohibition, and liquor not always readily available in bulk, there was a shortage of Scotch whiskey in the royal Bundi cellars that year, so we made do with champagne for five nights. My wife's birthday happened to come on one of the five days, and by His Highness' graciousness it was certainly the most bang-up celebration she ever had.

The climax of the festivities was His Highness' formal birthday dinner in the massive dining hall of the old palace. This was, as Lord Mountbatten was moved to remark on a corresponding occasion several years before, indeed like a scene from the Arabian Nights. For this dinner His Highness reproduces as far as possible the court of the old days, when there was no electricity to light the noble old fortress-palace, and transportation to the hilltop where it stands was by sedan chair borne by picturesquely uniformed servants.

While the men proceeded partway up the steep hill overlooking Bundi town by jeep, then walked the remaining half mile or so of winding stone steps, the ladies were carried in the ancient palanquins. The way was lighted by a serpentine of flickering torches, and at the towering gates we were guided to the banquet hall by retainers dressed in the court costume of medieval Rajputana, of the days when Bundi was a great and powerful state.

Inside the palace was illuminated by hundreds of candles. At the banquet table, behind each chair a servant kept the hot, still air moving pleasantly by gently waving a huge, graceful fan of ostrich feathers studded with precious gems. After dinner, with the guests being entertained by exhibitions of classic Rajput swordplay, it was as Mountbatten had said, a night from another age.

It was at this dinner that most of us tasted *asha* for the first time. This is a super-charged Rajput drink, rather like a liqueur, whose ingredients include sheep's brains, ground bones and gold dust.

When enough *asha* was consumed, the results were as could have been expected. The banquet ended with a visiting Hollywood movie producer leading the other guests in "Hap-py birth-day, Ma-ha-ra-jah, hap-py birth-day to yooou!"

6

"Good Night, Sweet Prince"

PRINCELY EXTRAVAGANCE, LIKE PRINCELY WEALTH, IS GREATLY exaggerated in the popular conception. Over the years, readers of magazines and newspaper supplements have come to think of the Indian rulers as pampered, overfed wastrels with pockets full of jewels to be handed out to lady friends, fleets of Rolls-Royces, private pleasure yachts on the Mediterranean, sumptuous villas on the Riviera, ivory palaces with limitless harems, and so on, all paid for by taxes ground from a miserable and tyrannized peasantry. Enough of such stories are true to give the entire Princely Order an odious name, especially in India, where such excesses have been observed at firsthand.

There was the wedding, for instance, in a Rajput state, where a fountain in the palace garden spouted French vintage champagne instead of water at the reception. The Nawab of Junagadh, who was a dog fancier to an hysterical extent, was estimated to have spent fifty thousand dollars on a "wedding reception" at the mating of a prize bitch. The late, often-married Maharajah of Kapurthala, a Francophile whose palace, where French is the court language, is a smaller duplicate of Versailles, and the Gaekwar of Baroda, since deposed, were among the most spectacular playboys in Europe in their time. The Maharajah of Kashmir, now also deposed, was the central figure as "Mr. A" in England's most famous blackmail case. Another ruler, still living, was deposed for implication in the murder of a dancing girl. The late Maharajah of Alwar lost his throne when he climaxed an outrageous life by setting fire to a polo pony that had displeased him, after dousing the animal with gasoline. Such notorious cases came to make the title "maharajah" synonymous with scandalous living and opulence.

Before India became independent and the government took a socialist turn, even the more conservative rulers indulged in display that no prince has dared to attempt since 1947. When a potentate visiting New Delhi dined out, it was customary for him to take over an entire restaurant, barring the public. His own cooks and servants replaced the regular staff for the evening, and used His Highness' own silver and dinner service. They carried huge retinues wherever they went.

The Nizam of Hyderabad is credited with the record in this regard, the story being told of him in his younger days that when he paid a state visit to the Nawab of Rampur in his special train, he brought along three hundred concubines. "I thought the ladies might appreciate an outing," he is said to have explained to the astounded Nawab.

Even today, with their powers gone and their purses clipped, many of the princes maintain the façade of reigning royalty, keeping aides-de-camp on hand twenty-four hours a day, in shifts, to light their cigarettes, order drinks, and see to any other of His Highness' routine wants. In their palaces and suites they are still treated like the absolute monarchs they once were, with retainers backing out of the royal presence bowing almost to the floor, and so on. But these pretenses are no longer paraded, and the average Indian today is not likely to come in contact with this anachronistic way of life unless he is himself situated near the palace. In the latter case, it is more than possible that he would not disapprove, for the princes have by no means entirely lost their old grip on the imagination and reverence of their former subjects.

What the public, especially abroad, has heard of a few Indian princes is unfair to many others, who have been brought up from infancy to feel their responsibility toward their subjects. I have talked to many rulers, before and after they lost their powers, who certainly appeared to have a sincere preoccupation with the welfare of their people. In any case, when there were 562 of them, they couldn't all have been bad, and I'm sure a majority of them weren't.

It is another misconception that all Indian princes were fabulously wealthy. It is true that a ruler who turned back half the state revenue for public purposes was considered an enlightened monarch—he had complete control of the treasury and could keep it all! But of the 562 states, some were so poor that if the prince had kept all the money that came in, he still wouldn't have had much. In other cases, the rulers felt no necessity to try to build up private fortunes, since all their wants, however extravagant, were fulfilled from state funds at the royal nod. Some of these now have no resources but their privy purses, or pensions, which are in danger of being cut off any time.

The upcoming generation of princelings is thinking in terms of gainful careers, in government service, farming or business. Several former reigning princes have gone into the Indian diplomatic service, where their foreign educations and polished manners are of considerable value. The Raja of Faridkot is one of India's leading big-scale farmers. Some others, not entirely to the Congress government's pleasure, have gone successfully into politics.

His Highness the Maharajadhiraj of Darbhanga, one of the biggest landowners in India until much of his holdings were nationalized, is said to be the banker of the princes. He is believed to be at least the fourth richest man in India still—the Nizam, the Maharajah of Bikaner, and the Maharajah of Gwalior are said to be ahead of him—and no doubt would stand high in a chart of the wealthiest individuals in the world. It is said that his jewels alone, which include the Marie Antoinette necklace and the famous Naulakha Emerald, are worth forty million dollars, but probably no one knows. His business interests are widespread, reaching into many of India's leading industries. And he really looks like the popular conception of an Indian potentate, with an enormous paunch, bristling black mustaches, and a huge diamond in each ear lobe.

The town of Darbhanga, in Bihar state near the Nepal border, is tumble-down, miserable and smelly. On the edge of it stands The Raj, a vast, walled estate that seemed approximately the size of Central Park in New York City. It contains lakes, temples, palaces, guest houses, parade grounds and administration buildings, all in red sandstone and in keeping with the chaste Indo-Saracenic architecture of the crenelated wall and the massive entrance gates, which resemble those of the famous Mogul tombs and forts of Delhi and Agra.

All this is the private estate of the Maharajadhiraj Sri Kameshwar Singh. Among the gewgaws collected there in the last two and a half centuries are such varied playthings as the ceremonial coach, all solid silver including the wheels, meant to be drawn by two elephants; and, in the main palace throne room, a set of distorting "fun mirrors" such as one sees at amusement parks. (The palace of the Kings of Nepal in Katmandu also has a dozen such mirrors, imported from Czechoslovakia and toted over the mountains on the backs of coolies.) The Darbhanga palace also abounds in stuffed tigers. His Highness' shoots are famous; in this part of the country tigers are hunted on elephants. Incidentally, riding an elephant bareback may look romantic, but it isn't, for the pachyderms have very sharp spines.

The Maharajadhiraj of Darbhanga is a rarity, a Brahmin prince, which gives him double power with the people. But the Darbhanga family is not a ruling dynasty. An ancestor, the story goes, fell out of the good graces of the British for insisting that a foreigner addressing him must not only stand a respectful number of paces away, but also must be downwind, so that the breeze would not sully the Brahmin with the pollution of a noncaste person's presence.

It turned out that not being a ruling prince was the most fortunate thing that could have happened to Kameshwar Singh. As he was a private citizen, although with a title, his jewels and property indisputably belonged to him, whereas in the case of reigning princes the New Delhi government could claim that most of their wealth belonged not to the Maharajah as an individual but to the state, and thereby deprive him of it unless he could establish his right to a hardhearted States Ministry.

And that is how the Maharadhiraj of Darbhanga happens to be the princes' banker.

The 562 princely realms of united India varied in size from vast domains like Kashmir and Hyderabad, each larger than England and Scotland together, down to tiny enclaves of a few acres. They came into existence in various ways. Some were very ancient states. Others, like Hyderabad, were suzerains that gradually established their independence from the central power, in Hyderabad's case the Mogul court at Delhi. Sometimes a local warrior or bandit leader simply marked out some territory for himself and had the power to make it stick. Some of the smaller states came into being when they were presented by a great ruler to a retainer as a reward for some service.

The Wali of Swat, a mountain state now belonging to Pakistan, achieved his ruling status as late as the middle 1920's, when the British governors of the wild Northwest Frontier suddenly woke up to the fact that the Wali, a Moslem tribal leader, was well on the way to creating another Afghanistan under their noses. They recognized him as a ruler in return for his pledge not to extend his territories across the Indus River.

The unique title of Wali originated this way: the monarch-to-be of Swat wanted to be called Shah, but this the British rejected in deference to the Shah of Persia; he then suggested Sultan, but that conflicted with the Sultan of Turkey, not to mention Babe Ruth; he rejected Nawab as a title not of sufficient dignity; so they settled on Wali, a Persian word meaning ruler or leader. But his subjects addressed him as "Badshah Sahib," which is like saying "Mister King." He was a descendant of the famous Moslem religious leader, the Akhund of Swat, of whom a famous verse was written:

> Who, or why, or which, or what
> Is the Akhund of Swat?

The old Wali, who made himself a kingdom by consolidating the wild tribes through every device called for including murder, only met his match once, in the person of the great photographer, Margaret Bourke-White. The story was told me when I visited Swat the first time in 1948.

The hardy old mountain potentate, though in his middle sixties, made it a daily practice to climb a 1,000-foot hill behind his palace every morning. Miss Bourke-White wanted a picture of this, but she could never get the Wali in a pose that satisfied her. Looking for just the right angle and setting, she kept him stumping from crag to crag, until finally the Wali turned helplessly to his aides and demanded in Pushtu, "What in the name of Allah is this woman doing to me?" A picture later appeared in *Life*.

After running his state singlehanded for a number of years, settling all questions personally through a direct telephone system linking the palace at Saidu Sharif with the forts he had built in every corner of the realm, the Wali abdicated in favor of his son. This was his way of insuring an orderly succession. Unable to write his name, but a wise and progressive ruler after having been a brave and wily warrior in many fierce tribal skirmishes, the original Wali was the last of an era in the untamed Frontier region. With modern administration under Karachi fast overtaking the tribes, his like will probably never be seen again.

Not all rulers were absolute, like the Wali, with power of life and death over their subjects. Some were hardly more than licensed tax collectors with certain administrative and judicial functions. Many of the pettier states were really "estates," the ruler exercising only a landlord's rights. The various treaties and agreements with the British, as the Paramount Power above all the rulers, were of infinite variety. But in the principal states the ruler was at least nominally an absolute monarch in his own territory, having ceded to the British control only over defense, communications and foreign affairs. In practice, however, the British held the reins through a resident Political Officer, who advised the ruler.

There was little actual interference with a native ruler, however eccentric he might be, until his misdeeds or maladministration went beyond all tolerance, as in some of the cases cited. Ordinarily the British interest lay in keeping the princes content, and through them maintaining order in nearly half of India's territory and a third of the population. The princes themselves were kept softened with honors and flattery.

While the Congress and the Moslem League were debating partition with the British, many wondered what would be the place of the princely states in a free India. There was a variety of ideas.

Many of the rulers thought in terms of complete independence for their states. One or two of the more powerful princes, notably the Nizam of Hyderabad, tentatively suggested a Dominion status within the British Commonwealth. A proposal that received serious attention, at least in the press, was for a federation of princely states to form a third country, separate from India and Pakistan, to be known as Rajasthan (the name has no connection, except in definition, with the state of Rajasthan later formed within the Indian Union by consolidating the Rajput territories).

The rulers had their own deliberative body, called the Chamber of Princes, presided over at this time by the Nawab of Bhopal. There was a vague thought among all the princes that they should get together in their own interest, but ancient dynastic rivalries and jealousies had the effect of precluding any kind of common front. A web of family feuds dating back to all-but-forgotten wars, broken alliances, and treacheries of the distant past still colors the princes' personal relations with each other.

When independence came to India and Pakistan in August 1947, the princely states were simply cast loose by the British to make their own arrangements with the two new Dominions. To those who relied on their old and honored treaties with Britain to protect them from the hostile colossus of Congress-ruled India that suddenly rose all around them, London blandly replied that with the withdrawal of the British Raj, paramountcy automatically lapsed, and the states' treaties were no longer in force. The Princes, whose dynasties had faithfully stood behind the British in time after time of need, regarded this repudiation as an arrant breach of faith, but that is how it had to be.

Mountbatten, whose royal family connections earned him a special respect from the Indian princes, called a meeting of rulers in New Delhi and laid down the alternatives open to them. There were only two: declare their independence, or accede to either India or Pakistan. Mountbatten, as a practical man, strongly advised the second course, and indeed there was no other that would have withstood the temper of the times.

With the Congress governments in New Delhi and the provinces continually agitating against the princes, ready to suborn and support sedition within their realms if necessary, and capable finally—as was to be demonstrated in more than one instance—of taking over states by military force, no ruler was in an advantageous position to bargain for independence. However, several princes were poorly advised and didn't seem to realize the weakness of their position, and for them the results were sad.

What Mountbatten apparently had in mind for the princes was accession to one Dominion or the other by an agreement similar to those that had governed the states' relation to the British Raj; that is, the rulers would give over control of defense, communications and foreign affairs, and in all other respects would remain autonomous. Most of the princes plainly saw that refusal would mean speedy ruin, and readily entered into the suggested relationship with the appropriate Dominion government.

Later, about three weeks before the scheduled date for the British withdrawal, Mountbatten warned the princes that the majority of their states were "irretrievably linked geographically" with India, and that they must sign with New Delhi. There were hardly a dozen of the states that were not surrounded by, or contiguous to, Indian territory. Religion was to be another factor in the ruler's choice. As Mountbatten pointed out, it would be to the interest of the states with predominantly Hindu populations to accede to India, while Moslem states adjoining Pakistani territory should join Pakistan.

In regard to nine Moslem states in the West there was no argument from the New Delhi government, and they acceded to Pakistan as a matter of course.

In the large southern state of Travancore, the young Maharajah suggested that his possession of a long sea coast, with ports and foreign trade, qualified him to assert independence. But after some baring of teeth from New Delhi, other counsels prevailed and Travancore came meekly into the Union. But Kashmir and Hyderabad, the two largest states, were still thinking matters over. Both were destined to become not only an Indian but an international concern.

Meanwhile, the Moslem Nawab of Junagadh abruptly exercised what he conceived to be his sovereign right, and acceded to Pakistan although the majority of his subjects were Hindus and his state was not only surrounded by Indian territory but was cut up into no fewer than thirteen separate parcels with Indian corridors between. The nearby, smaller state of Manavadar, which was in a comparable situation, followed Junagadh's lead. Pakistan promptly opened an airline from Karachi to this enclave within India, and New Delhi was furious at this violation of the Mountbatten doctrine.

With Indian encouragement, a party of Hindus rebelled against the Nawab and appealed to New Delhi for troops to restore order in the state. The Indian government wasted little time before sending a force by sea. The Nawab fled to Karachi, and India ostentatiously held a plebiscite. As was not unexpected, the vote was more than 90 per cent in India's favor, so New Delhi officially annexed the state. Manavadar fell to India incidentally. Pakistan lodged a protest with the Security Council of the United Nations, charging India with aggression, but the matter never reached the discussion stage and is conceded to be as good as dead.

Hyderabad was also surrounded by Indian territory. But the Nizam, as the ruler of a state larger than many sovereign nations and with a population of eighteen million—more than Canada and Australia together—claimed a special position and refused to be hurried. He told New Delhi, in effect, "You are not dealing with a puny little princeling now, but with the ruler of a sizable nation with its own currency, stamps and army."

The Nizam's army went on the alert, and guns and ammunition were flown in from abroad. The potentate sent envoys to New Delhi, to deal with India as one sovereign state to another. Proposals and counterproposals were exchanged in a wearying succession of official notes, while normal relations continued under a one-year "standstill agreement" to maintain the status quo pending a solution. Despite the standstill agreement India gradually tightened an economic blockade around the landlocked state.

Of the eighteen million people in Hyderabad, about two million were Moslems; the rest were almost all Hindus, including the important phallic-worshiping Lingayat sect. The problem swiftly assumed a religious complexion. Although the Moslems of Hyderabad were relatively few, they included the ruler, and the state was looked upon as a center of Islamic culture and the last vestige of the Mogul Empire. Urdu, the *lingua franca* developed by the Moguls and written in Arabic script, was the official state language, although the bulk of the population spoke Canarese, Marathi and Telegu. And Osmania University, founded by the Nizam, was a great center of Islamic learning. For these reasons the Moslems of Hyderabad, with vociferous support from Pakistan, opposed merger with India as another Hindu move against Islam. But perhaps a more important motive was the favored position of the Moslem minority, who had a near-monopoly on state services.

The communal aspect of the situation was brought to the fore by the Moslems themselves, and they played into New Delhi's hands. A fanatical Moslem organization called the Razakars, headed by a bearded zealot named Qasim Razvi, took such a militant stand that the government of India soon was able to make a case that Hindus were being made the victims of coercion and violence. Armed Razakars were also accused of raiding villages in Indian territory. The Indian government radio, and the newspapers, soon had an inflammatory propaganda campaign in full swing, alleging that the state of Hyderabad was beset by widespread outlawry.

In September, 1948, India sent troops into Hyderabad to "restore order." The Nizam's army, despite its previous bluster, wisely offered only token resistance, and the state was taken in a few days.

With the investment of Hyderabad by the Indian Army, the Nizam meekly acceded to the Union. Later, he said that he had wished all along to come to terms with New Delhi, but had been misled by his advisors. At any rate, that was the end of the Nizam's rule, though he was allowed to remain on his throne and was eventually designated as the Rajpramukh or constitutional head of the state. Except for the nationalization of his vast land holdings, he was permitted to retain his great wealth, but its handling was placed under supervision. He was granted a privy purse of $2,100,000 a year, in rupees.

The capitulation of Hyderabad had symbolic significance as the end of long Moslem rule in the Deccan, as that part of India is called. As in the case of Junagadh, Pakistan took a complaint to the United Nations, but again the protest was never acted upon.

In the end, the Nizam's intransigeance did not leave him any worse off than his brother princes. In the matter of the privy purse, he has the largest of all. The privy purse varies according to the importance of the ruler, some amounting to several hundred thousand dollars a year, others being merely token payments to petty chiefs. In principle, the privy purse is the Indian government's return to the prince for ceding his powers. There is a nationwide agitation to abolish these generous pensions, which are guaranteed in perpetuity by the constitution of India, and the princes themselves don't think they are going to last much longer.

So far, Prime Minister Nehru has defended the privy purse as a sacred obligation. This expenditure costs the Indian exchequer approximately thirteen million dollars a year, but Nehru and others have argued that this is a small price for the peaceful acquisition of the princely territories, totaling nearly half the entire land area of the country.

From the point of view of the princes, their pensions are not extravagant considering the extent of their obligations. Most of them have hordes of relatives dependent upon them for support—a prince whose grandfather was a polygamist might have to provide for half a dozen grandmothers and any number of aunts. Their palace establishments are no longer kept up by state funds, but must be supported out of the prince's pockets. To abandon this costly outlay would mean turning legions of faithful servitors out of their homes and livelihood.

After the death of the incumbent prince, the privy purse of his successors will be limited to a maximum of $200,000 a year. But few if any princes have any faith in the sanctity of the government's pledge, especially since Nehru, who has been their defender, himself proposed in 1953 that the one hundred two princes receiving privy purses of $20,000 or more should take a voluntary cut.

In the original deal with the rulers, New Delhi guaranteed the perpetuation of their titles, their right to personal flags and other dignities and honors such as the receiving of gun salutes and the privilege of being addressed as "Your Highness." But since the articles of accession were signed, the status of the princes has been whittled down so steadily that it would appear to be only a question of time until they are deprived even of their hereditary titles, and become in every way ordinary citizens.

The princely states were allowed to remain autonomous for only a few months. Then the States Ministry began to study the administrative problems created by the presence of 562 separate jurisdictions, each with its own customs barriers, many with their own stamps and coinage, and a multiplicity of legal codes. A number of the states were not even in one piece, but consisted of scattered enclaves within other states, and enclaves within enclaves.

Consolidation of the states was in the charge of V. P. Menon, a distinguished civil servant who had been Mountbatten's constitutional advisor, described by the last Viceroy as "the one man who had most to do with the mechanics of partition." K. M. Panikkar, later Ambassador to Communist China and Egypt and a master intrigant, had the job of keeping the rulers apart while Menon sharpened his ax. Panikkar had served several princes as *dewan*, or Prime Minister, and knew exactly how to play upon their personalities and jealousies so that they would never get together in defense of the powers still left to them.

Menon, besides being extremely skillful in administrative statecraft, was peculiarly well suited temperamentally for his assignment to smash the princes.

"When I came up here years ago, a poor boy from Malabar," he related in his office one day, "I went into a shop one day and watched a Maharani buy a hundred expensive saris. Another time I was present when a Maharajah walked into a sporting goods store and casually ordered a hundred thousand rupees' worth of hunting rifles. And one day, on one of my civil service assignments, I was stopped at fifteen different state customs posts on a thirty-mile drive through Kathiawar. I thought it was time this sort of nonsense was stopped."

Menon's program was to merge the smaller states into larger, more manageable units, if they were contiguous, or into an existing province when they were, as was often the case, tiny dots surrounded by provincial territory. It was left to Menon to persuade each prince to this step, which to the ruler meant nothing less than surrendering his ruling powers and the political identity of his ancestral kingdom. How successful he was could be measured from the ensuing series of modest newspaper items, each series running about like this:

First, a small headline, "Mr. V. P. Menon Visits State of Chhota Hazri";

Then, in the Governor-General's daily Court Circular, a brief notice, "H.H. the Maharajah of Chhota Hazri has arrived";

And soon, a banner headline, "CHHOTA HAZRI MERGED!"

The 489 petty states of Kathiawar, where Menon had his experience with the customs barriers, were merged first, into one state of Saurashtra, with the premier prince, the famous Jam Saheb of Nawanagar, as Rajpramukh. In the end, only six princely states remained as single political units: Mysore and Hyderabad, because their size made them viable; Manipur, Tripura, and Cutch, because of their strategic geographical situation on the borders, where it was desirable to have the territory under central control from New Delhi; and Bhopal, by a special arrangement with the Nawab. When the state boundaries of India are redrawn to take account of linguistic interests, some of these may also be broken up.

As the princely territories became parts of provinces (now called states), the wealth of the rulers came under examination by Mr. Menon.

The States Ministry began its study of princely property on the principle that everything the ruler owned belonged not to him personally but to his state, unless he could sustain a claim that the wealth had been acquired through investment or some other legitimate means by himself or an ancestor. Jewelry was impounded immediately, and declared to be state treasures, but the ruler was appointed custodian of the jewels and was permitted to wear them on state occasions when their appearance was traditional. But he could not sell them. The extravagant fleets of automobiles were confiscated, except whatever number, to a maximum of five, that the Ministry decided the prince needed for his establishment. A prince might have many palaces, and lodges and villas all over India; he was allowed to retain one palace in his state, and one other house, either in the mountains or at the seashore.

The princes, being thrown entirely on their personal resources and a limited privy purse of uncertain permanence, were more than glad to let the new government take over expensive palaces and guest houses, many of which were immediately converted into hotels. The rulers urged the successor authorities to take over their voracious herds of ceremonial elephants; at one time during this period it was possible to buy an elephant for $60—but it would cost $5,000 a year to feed him.

With their purses trimmed, the princes had to reduce their standard of living drastically. Out went the troops of dancing girls, the palace orchestras, the lavish shooting parties (nowadays some princes put on tiger shoots for pay, with an eye on the American tourist trade), the open-handed gifts.

An unfortunate by-product of the clipping of the princes' wings was the loss of generous princely support to philanthropies and the arts. Sport suffered, too; for example, the Maharajah of Jaipur had to cut his string of polo ponies from one hundred twenty to forty. "Jai" is one of those who is still doing all right.

Whether the princes were good or bad rulers, they seemed to fill a need in the lives of their peoples. The Indians in the states were accustomed to personal rule, and they loved the pageantry of the royal processions and *durbars* that brought the only color into their lives. When democracy took over, the new idea was distinctly on trial. Naturally, many were quick to seize upon any flaw in the Congress government, and contrast the new order unfavorably with the old.

Under the princes, most of the states' peoples had no conditioning in self-government. The rulers generally followed the practice of bringing in *dewans* and other officials from outside, sometimes hiring Britons. As should be expected, such a system of government often worked more efficiently than the cumbersome processes of democracy, and it can still be seen today that numerous princely states are ahead of the rest of India in good roads, schools, hospitals, and public health. Some states, of course, were exceptionally backward even for India.

As the princes stepped out, the Congress party came in. It is a general condition, true all over India, that apart from a few exceptional men like Morarji Desai, chief minister of Bombay State, the average Congressite was little skilled in administration. He had devoted his life to the struggle against the British, and so had acquired a minimum of training for actual government. Also, having given their best years to a cause, many were inclined to sit back and enjoy the fruits.

The Congressmen of the princely states, by and large, were without doubt the least equipped of all for their suddenly assumed responsibilities. More capable men sent in from outside were resented as "carpetbaggers." What the peoples of the states still think of the Congress has been shown in elections, in which independent candidates backed by the princes

—sometimes the princes themselves were candidates—easily defeated the Congress professionals.

These conditions can be expected to change. Meanwhile, the princes, in most if not all of the many states I have visited, still reign in their former subjects' hearts.

"In His Highness' day," a peasant once said, "if anyone, no matter how poor, had a grievance he could go to the palace and be received in audience. Any subject could go up to His Highness when he traveled about the country, and tell him his troubles. And if His Highness saw fit, he would issue an order and something was done, at once. Now what goes on? Every time you have anything to do with government, you fill out papers in quadruplicate, the wretched lawyers take all your money, and nothing ever happens. How is it better? The Congress-wallas tell us that our taxes, instead of going to His Highness, will be spent on schools, roads, hospitals. May I ask, where are they? No, it was better in His Highness' time."

This is an extreme view, but it does represent many.

The esteem in which the people still hold their princes can be observed any time the former ruler goes abroad in his own state. I was particularly impressed with an experience in Indore, where I happened to ride to an official function—it was the opening of a community development project—in the same car with the Maharajah and the Maharani Fay, his charming and beautiful California wife.

The road was lined with bowing subjects, and His Highness had to stop the car every few hundred feet to receive garlands of flowers. After the ceremony, the Maharajah and I drove unannounced into a typical village of narrow, unpaved streets and mud huts. The village went wild. Every window and rooftop was crowded with men, women, and children who showered the car with flowers, and the streets were made impassable by villagers of all ages who pushed and jostled just to touch the Maharajah's car. I never saw even Nehru given a reception like that.

7

Paradise with "Full Sprang Seats"

His Highness the Maharajah Sir Hari Singh, horse race-loving despot of Jammu and Kashmir, also nursed dreams of maintaining an independent monarchy. His remote and beautiful mountain state, extending from the burning plains of the Punjab to majestic heights of the Himalayas and Karakorams, was thus destined to become an international hot potato and a real threat to peace in Asia. The ruler's shilly-shallying was also to cost him his throne.

For helping the British in the Sikh wars, the Maharajah's grandfather was permitted to buy Kashmir for the equivalent of about two million dollars. This turned out to be one of the greatest real estate bargains in history. The state is about the size of Minnesota, and the beauty of its lakes and mountains, often compared to those of Switzerland, made it one of the favorite vacation spots in all Asia. Mention of the Vale of Kashmir conjures a vision of tranquil loveliness the world over. In the United Nations councils, the name was to come to connote intransigeance and strife.

Srinagar, the capital of Kashmir (the state is properly Jammu and Kashmir, but in general usage just Kashmir), is a fourteen-hundred-year-old city still medieval in appearance, especially as viewed from the river Jhelum, which bisects it. The ramshackle multistoried buildings, reached by stairways up the towering retaining walls along the river bank, give the city a breath of antiquity that is not spurious. In Srinagar one begins to get the feeling of being in Central Asia, and it is easy to imagine oneself transported centuries back, when the bazaars along the river were an important trade mart on the caravan routes from Cathay to the Middle East. Kashmir is bounded by China, Tibet, India, Pakistan, and Afghanistan, and the border comes within twenty miles of Russian territory. Wares from all these countries, and Iran as well, may be found in the hundreds of dusty shops along the river.

Here is where the Great Mogul came for the summer, with a retinue of thousands, and built the world-famous garden of Shalimar. This, and other formal gardens equally beautiful, are leading tourist attractions today.

There is a legend, I have been told, among some Moslems of Kashmir that when Christ arose on the third day after His Crucifixion, he did not ascend directly to Heaven but secretly made His way to the valley and there spent the remainder of His earthly days. Kashmir has often enough been described as a heaven on earth.

At a height just under a mile above sea level, the Vale has a delightful summer climate. For a stay of any length of time one takes a houseboat on the river or one of the several broad lakes. These flat-bottomed craft are nothing less than swanky apartments afloat. Each has a forward veranda, from which to view the floating lotus gardens, the constantly intriguing passage of all manner of native boats, or the peace of the distant snow-capped peaks. The veranda opens into a spacious living room, entirely furnished even to books in the bookcases. There will be a separate dining room, and any number of bedrooms, each with its private bath. The top deck is ordinarily fixed as a garden for sunbathing. This description is of a typical boat.

Moored astern will be a separate cook boat, with the kitchen and quarters for the servants, who will probably all be of the same family. The cook will be an expert in his art, capable of learning to prepare any dish that he doesn't already know. The only drawback is that there will be no beef, as the Hindu Maharajah has decreed a stiff penalty for killing cows, or even bringing tinned beef into the state; and pork is also unknown, because all the servants are Moslems and won't touch it. So one makes out somehow on mutton, lamb, venison, chicken, duck, goose, and partridge.

The boat, the food, and the service will cost between three dollars and five dollars per person per day. For an extra fee to the pole coolies, you can have the boat moved to another place any time you get tired of the view. Most of your travel to the town and to points of interest will be by gondola-like taxi boats called *shikara*, each advertising "full sprang seats."

In the *shikara*, which is propelled by a crew wielding heart-shaped paddles, you lie Roman-fashion on rich cushions, piled on top of these "full sprang seats," and if you feel like being a lotus-eater literally, you can reach out and pluck one as you glide through the floating gardens. (It's a rich-tasting plant, the lotus, at least raw it is.) From the names of the *shikara*, "Night of Love," and so on, you will correctly deduce that Srinagar was an American G.I. rest camp during the war. The names of many shops are equally intriguing in a different way: Suffering Moses, Cash Helen, Abdullah the Worst, World's Worst Embroidery Shop, to name a few.

It is not necessary to tour the shops. All the wares in town will be brought to you by the merchants themselves in *shikara*, and a great deal of the time the deck of your house-boat living room will be covered with beautiful silks, embroideries, furs, jeweled knickknacks, and the famous Kashmir shawls that can be pulled through a ring. This will be fun for about three days, and then the constant importunities of the endless stream of water-going merchants will become a nuisance. The Kashmiri salesman is the most persistent in the world. He will insist, sometimes in tears, that "you don't have to buy, Huzur, just look—no buy, just look, these beautiful thing!" And until you've been there long enough to develop a heart of granite, you will find it virtually impossible to resist his blandishments.

After several visits to Kashmir, one lasting a full month during which my wife, Jean, and I must have bought one of everything, I thenceforth felt it my duty to society to warn all intending visitors that merchants nowhere are more charming, or more undependable, than in the enchanted Vale. "Let the buyer beware" should be the motto, and he had better be sure of what he is buying, particularly in furs and jewels, if he is not to discover too late that he has been charmingly cheated. The best guide on prices is to check first at the Kashmir Government Emporium, where there is a sample of practically everything for sale. And any fraud should be reported to the tourist office, which will swiftly set matters right and scare the offending merchant out of his wits.

That incredibly low price for your houseboat idyll can also be a snare. The visitor is advised by the government tourist office to ascertain beforehand exactly what is included. If you don't, you will find the final bill swollen unmercifully by all sorts of charges for "extras." These may include mosquito netting, a bottle of catsup, a roll of toilet paper, anything the head boatman can think of that isn't on the list and that you might use. A tip is customary, but have a firm understanding with the boatman beforehand that you are going to give him ten per cent of the bill when you leave, and that he, not you, will do the distributing among the subordinate staff. Then, if you have been pleased by the service, add a little more. And you will still, no matter what you do, have a big argument on your hands when you come to settle! But it is all worth it.

When I first visited Kashmir in October, 1947, the houseboats were empty and the merchants were selling frantically at fantastic bargains, because a looting, murdering army of fierce Pathan tribesmen on the warpath was only five miles from the city, and the terrified capital expected a flaming doom any hour.

Under the Mountbatten formula, Kashmir might have been expected to accede to Pakistan. The population of the state, about four million, is 78 per cent Moslem, and more of the state border adjoins Pakistan than India. Three rivers flowing out of Kashmir, the Indus, Jhelum and Chenab, are vital to the agricultural economy of West Pakistan. Except for Jammu province, the state is wholly inaccessible to India except by air and by one treacherous mountain road which is closed by snow in the winter. Kashmir's natural trade routes all run into Pakistan, although the chief Kashmiri products—silks, carpets, papier-mâché, leather, embroidery ware, fine woodwork, ornaments of precious metals and gems, furs, and fruits—find their principal market through India.

In what Karachi took to be an acknowledgment of the state's links to Pakistan, the Maharajah, at the time of partition, signed a "standstill agreement" with the Moslem Dominion. Under these terms Pakistan held the responsibility for the Kashmir posts and telegraphs and other obligations previously devolving on the government of undivided India. Karachi assumed that this step would be a prelude to accession.

The decision on accession in all the states rested solely with the ruler. Constitutionally, there was no question of consulting the wishes of the population, for whatever attributes of sovereignty the states possessed were vested entirely in the ruling prince. Pakistanis were confident, however, that since the people of Kashmir were overwhelmingly Moslem, the Hindu Maharajah would take into account the opinion of his subjects, which again was assumed to be unquestionably in favor of accession to Pakistan.

But from New Delhi, persuasions were being exercised on the Maharajah to accede to India. Nehru, himself of Kashmiri ancestry, had taken a keen interest in the state. Sheikh

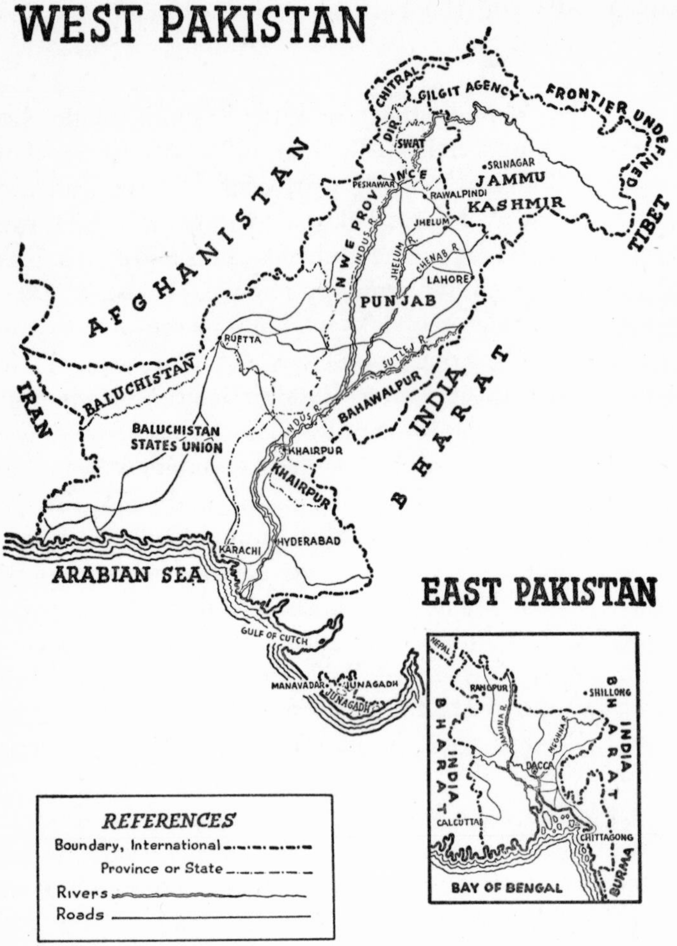

Mohammed Abdullah, head of the National Conference party opposed to the Maharajah's rule, was the Indian Premier's close friend of many years. Nehru once was arrested in Kashmir when he went there to support the Sheikh's cause. But there was a more important reason for Nehru's desire to annex Kashmir than the accident of his ancestry and his friendship for Sheikh Abdullah.

Nehru has consistently refused to acknowledge that the

partition of India was made on a religious basis. He prefers to describe the split as the "secession" of certain territories, now forming Pakistan, as the result of "local political self-determination." It seems obvious that Nehru persists loudly in this highly doubtful premise as an appeal to the loyalty of the Moslems still in India. It is for the same reason, more than for sentiment, and certainly not through any desire to add the sizable economic problems of Kashmir to India's already overburdened economy, that Nehru is determined Kashmir shall be Indian.

In short, Nehru reasons that if predominantly Moslem Kashmir joins predominantly Hindu India, the fact will reassure the none-too-happy Moslems already in India. But if the Kashmiris were to attach themselves to Pakistan, this would tend to confirm the religious basis of the "two-nation theory," and would add to the uneasiness of Indian Moslems. And India's extremist Hindu elements would probably seize upon the loss of Kashmir as an excuse to bait the despised Moslems. The result could easily be another disastrous religious uprising and migration, not only of Hindus from Kashmir but of Moslems from India. It is thought less likely that the docile Kashmiri Moslems, their spirits tamed by many invasions and oppressions, would flee their homes under Indian rule.

The Moslems in the district of Poonch, in the western part of Jammu province, do not happen to share the tractability of the usual downtrodden Kashmiri peasant. A rather poor area for agriculture, Poonch contributed thousands of men to the British Indian Army, for they share the famous martial qualities of the neighboring Punjabi Moslems. After the partition, former soldiers living in Poonch began to raise demonstrations in favor of accession to Pakistan. When their meetings were fired upon by the Maharajah's forces, they rose in rebellion and quickly put to flight the state troops, composed principally of Hindus of the Dogra caste. The undeclared war between India and Pakistan in Kashmir stemmed directly from this uprising through a series of related events.

Kashmiris, particularly Moslems, had good reason to hate the Maharajah's despotic rule. Numerous minor but annoying discriminations against Moslems and in favor of the Hindu minority were galling enough. More important, no state's people in India suffered more at the hands of a ruler than the miserably poor peasantry of Kashmir. Normal taxes, such as the levy on land, far exceeded the rates charged elsewhere. In addition to this special hardship, the Maharajah's government taxed at every conceivable excuse. Many Kashmiri peasants' homes have no windows, because of the special window tax. There was a tax on the hearth, too, which there was no escaping, because the whole of Kashmir is bitterly cold in winter. There was a tax on every wife, every domestic animal, every occupation. There was even a tax on chimneys.

While the fighting Moslems of Poonch were cutting down the Maharajah's troops, and incidentally mistreating the local Hindus, Sikh and Hindu refugees were pouring into Jammu. These homeless and destitute people, lusting to avenge the wrongs they had suffered at the hands of Moslems in West Pakistan, aroused their co-religionists in Jammu against their Moslem neighbors. At that time the size of the two communities was nearly even, the Moslems having a slight majority. The ensuing massacre and evacuation of Moslems, which lasted well over a month, changed the ratio and gave the non-Moslems a decided majority that they still hold.

As all this was taking place the fanatical Moslem tribes of the Frontier States—Swat, Dir and Chitral—and the tribal territory along the Afghan border heard the electrifying cry from Kashmir, "Islam in danger!" At once the fierce Maliks (chiefs) of the crags, the deserts and the mountains of the wild Northwest Frontier raised the terrible slogan of "Jehad" or holy war. Traditionally inclined toward banditry because of the poverty of their arid country, the tribesmen were far from unconscious of the rich loot to be taken in a powerful raid upon a helpless Kashmir. The time was convenient, for thousands of the tribesmen were already camped near the easily accessible Kashmir border, on their annual winter migration from their snowy homes to the milder plains.

The Pakistan government has steadfastly denied any official encouragement to the tribes in the invasion of Kashmir. It was not necessary to provide the tribesmen with arms, for they had been manufacturing their own for generations in factories hidden in their bleak mountain fastnesses. But there was never any doubt that Pakistani provincial authorities, perhaps unofficially but certainly not without the knowledge of Karachi, supplied the bloodthirsty tribal *lashkars* (war parties) with truck transport. And Pakistani Army officers, alleged to be on "leave," led the contingents.

Later, observers were to say that Pakistan made a serious mistake in letting operations fall into the hands of the ferocious Mahsud tribe. Looting, raping, killing, and burning, these fearsome warriors swept through Kashmir like a plague, until they reached the large town of Baramula, about twenty-five miles by good road from Srinagar. There they stopped a full night in a foolish quarrel over booty. The night's pause in Baramula changed history.

Meanwhile the Maharajah, on Indian advice, left his palace in Srinagar with truckloads of treasure, and fled to the town of Jammu, his winter capital. Sheikh Abdullah, who had been jailed for sedition and recently released, was asked to form a representative government.

As he was preparing to flee, the Maharajah implored New Delhi to send in troops to halt the raiders before they reached Srinagar. Lord Mountbatten, as Governor-General, replied that India could not legally put armed forces across the state border unless Kashmir acceded to the Indian Union. The ruler immediately acceded. And India at once mobilized all the air transport in the country to fly troops to Srinagar, which has the only airfield in the Vale.

The Indians arrived just in time to stop the raiders five miles from the capital. The delay overnight in Baramula, while Pakistani officers argued to convince the Maliks that Srinagar should not be looted, may have lost Pakistan the state, for if the invaders had pressed on they should have had possession of the airfield before the Indian troops could fly in. The only other access to the Vale would have been by one narrow road over the 10,000-foot Banihal Pass, soon to be closed by snow.

At this point the Indians made a serious political mistake that they were to regret ever after. Nehru made it a formal condition of accepting the Maharajah's accession to India that this action should be confirmed, after order had been restored, by ascertaining "the will of the people" of the state. Constitutionally, it was not necessary to do this, for the Maharajah's action, however it may have been contrived, legally and irrevocably handed the state over to India. How Nehru's idealistic gesture was to make Kashmir a powder keg for years to come would appear later.

Srinagar, one of the playgrounds of Asia, was a city of terror as the raiders closed in, except for the crusty, stout-hearted colony of retired British army officers and civil servants and their craggy, muscular wives. These were people who had given their lives to India, thirty-five and forty years, or more. Some had been born in India, of families who had served the Empire since the days of Clive. With India in the blood, and not belonging to England any more, they lived far better here than they could in Sussex or Kent on their small pensions, with their houseboats, their servants, and their dogs.

Their lives revolved around shooting, trekking, the Srinagar Club, and delayed copies of *The Times*. Tories all, they celebrated the Conservative victory in the 1947 elections with a big evening at the Club. "By Gad, sir," said an elderly retired major, thumping the floor with his cane, "England has come to her senses at last!"

With the advance of the raiders, who cruelly murdered an English family staying at a Catholic convent not far from Srinagar, the U. K. High Commission in New Delhi "got the wind up," as the British say. Special planes were "laid on" to evacuate the Britons from Srinagar, and most of the doughty group were reluctantly, heartbrokenly, making plans to go. Then came the question of evacuating their dogs—every retired Briton in India seems to have at least one dog, usually, for some reason, a dachshund. The dog problem changed the whole picture.

The U. K. High Commission was firm. Dogs would have to be left behind—animals could not be taken in the plane. There was consternation at the Srinagar Club.

"Not take my dog?" roared the old major, speaking for all. "Then, damn me, I'll not go! By gad, sir, I'll see it through!"

And see it through they did.

The Indian Army met the tribal *lashkars* on the outskirts of the city. The tribesmen are fierce hit-and-run fighters, excellent guerrillas, but they are not the type of soldier to stand and shoot it out, especially against a force of superior numbers and better arms, nor are they inclined toward disciplined military deployment. Meeting determined and methodical Indian opposition, they turned and ran. In a day or so the Indians had Baramula back, and correspondents went there to see what had happened.

We found Baramula almost a deserted city. Every shop and house had been so thoroughly plundered that I noticed not a single object of any use whatever left in the town.

There was not a skillet, not a pot or pan, not a teacup that had escaped the raiders. Every structure was completely stripped, left absolutely bare of everything; there was nothing left but plain walls and floors, with one exception: in one shop I did see, pasted on the wall, an old cover picture from *Life*. This was the only object left in the town that could have been removed. The Catholic church and convent where the British family had been killed, between Baramula and

Srinagar, had been wantonly wrecked, apparently in a religious frenzy reminiscent of Mahmud of Ghazni, whom the Hindus still call the "Idol Breaker." The Crucifix was torn down, the altar smashed, every statue demolished. All literature in the church and convent—hymnals, prayerbooks, tracts—had been torn and scattered. I had never seen the destructive work of religious fanatics before; this was like something out of the Dark Ages.

The Mahsuds, Afridis, and other tribesmen were expert looters. One British correspondent, Bill Sydney Smith of the London *Daily Express*, managed to get himself captured by the raiders, and experienced their work at firsthand. As Bill was taken by a wandering raiding party, he was seized and thrown down, but before he hit the ground, he said, he felt a dozen hands going into his pockets. In seconds he was stripped. His watch, wallet, everything disappeared into the pockets of the tribesmen. A Pakistani officer took charge of him before he could come to any physical harm, and Bill was eventually set free in Pakistan.

Bill Sydney Smith was responsible for another footnote to the history of the Kashmir war. One night, sitting in a bar in Rawalpindi, headquarters of the Pakistan Army and a jump-off point for the tribal raiders, Bill struck up a conversation with a young American, a rarity in those parts then. This was Russell Haight, a name soon to be briefly famous.

Haight had recently left his job with the Morrison-Knudsen Construction Company, an American outfit building roads and dams in Afghanistan. He was headed home at leisure, planning to wander through Pakistan, India and way points to Denver, where he lived. An unscheduled detour was ahead for this adventurous young man.

Talking with Bill Sydney Smith, Haight mentioned that he had been with three armies in the war, enlisting first with the Canadians, switching to the British with whom he made the commando raid at Dieppe, and finally transferring to the American Army when the U.S. came into the war.

The correspondent suggested that the raiders could use such an experienced soldier, and why didn't Haight apply to the Pakistanis for a commission? Haight thought it over and decided it was a good idea.

Pretty soon the world heard—first, of course, under Bill's by-line in the *Daily Express*—of Brigadier Russell Haight, the American soldier of fortune fighting with the tribesmen in Kashmir. By this time the pro-Pakistani Moslems of western Kashmir, from around Poonch, had formed their own Azad (free) Kashmir Provisional Government in opposition to Sheikh Abdullah's pro-Indian regime in Srinagar, and it was in the Azad Kashmir forces that Haight held his one-star commission. He saw some fighting, and was made commander of an embryo "International Brigade" consisting of himself, a couple of Anglo-Burmese, and one or two other nondescript foreigners at the beginning.

After a couple of months Haight got fed up with the suspicion and intrigues that soon surrounded his operations, culminating when someone took a surreptitious shot at him in a dark alley in Rawalpindi. At this time I was able to assist him in getting help from the American Embassy to fly back home. The State Department, never keen to have Americans involved in wars of other countries, was more than glad to expedite his departure by an American commercial plane out of Karachi.

Haight landed in New York in his green British-type uniform with the brigadier's pips, the Azad Kashmir shoulder flash in Urdu, and the towering Pathan turban on his blond head. After a try at insurance selling in Denver, he went back into the U.S. Army, served in Germany and Korea (where he was wounded twice), and now has the respected rank of first sergeant with a chestful of ribbons, a veteran of four armies at thirty-three.

8

The Highest War in History

THE WAR IN KASHMIR WAS ONE THAT A CORRESPONDENT COULD cover from both sides of the front lines. Many of us would fly to Srinagar, go out with the Indian forces, return to India, go over to Rawalpindi, cross the Kashmir border again on the Pakistan side, and do a turn with the Pakistanis. I refer to the forces fighting the Indians as Pakistanis because that is what they were, although the Pakistan Army was not in the war officially and as such until the summer of 1948. By that time United Nations observers, assigned to try to stop the hostilities, were on the spot, and the participation of Pakistani units could no longer be denied.

Karachi announced that these forces were sent into Kashmir only as the Indian troops were driving toward the border, and appeared about to threaten the integrity and security of Pakistan proper. Nehru had already charged Pakistan, in the U.N. Security Council, with "aggression" in Kashmir, and the admission that Pakistani regular forces were engaged now led to renewed and bitter accusations by the Indian leader.

Several years later Nehru was to take quite an opposite point of view on the entry of Communist Chinese troops into the Korean war. He refused to join in condemnation of Red China for aggression in this instance, arguing that the Peiping government was motivated by concern for the security of her borders as United Nations forces approached the Yalu River boundary. This was exactly the justification put forth by Pakistan for intervention in Kashmir.

Indian officials said privately that it was impossible to reason with Nehru on Kashmir.

"India may have been wrong on many things, but we are dead right on Kashmir," Nehru once told the Foreign Correspondents Association in New Delhi.

The war was energetically fought on both sides while it lasted, and it had many unique features. It was the war correspondent's dream assignment. One could take one's family to Srinagar and rent a houseboat on one of the gorgeous, cool lakes for the summer months, when Delhi was boiling under a pall of hot dust whisked from the nearby burning deserts by the dreaded *loo*. It was possible to alternate treks with the Indian Army, into the spectacular hills, with dreamy interludes on the lake. On the Pakistan side, too, coverage of this war was mostly a matter of interesting hikes with the tribesmen into valleys and passes of unsurpassed wild beauty, lunching *al fresco* with the turbanned, bearded Maliks on great ribs of sheep that one tore apart with one's fingers.

While covering the Pakistani side I managed to fly up to Gilgit and Skardu, near the borders of Russia and China. This was probably the scariest airplane ride in the world. There was a daily military run to these remote territories with supplies for the local garrisons. The planes were old Dakotas (C-47's) left behind by the U.S. Air Force after the war, and the pilots were daredevil Poles who had flown for Free Poland, then fought with the R.A.F., and now, men without a country, were in the service of Pakistan.

We took off from Peshawar, gateway to the Khyber Pass, as the sky was lightening before dawn. Seeing nothing interesting to look at on the monotonous Peshawar Plain, I stretched out on sacks of flour to sleep. About an hour later I awoke, gazed sleepily at the overhead for a while, then glanced out the window. Instantly I came wide awake, did a

Bob Hope double-take, and swallowed. We were flying up the narrow Indus Gorge, at seven or eight thousand feet, and the snow-capped mountains on both sides of us, so close that it sometimes seemed that the pilot had to bank to keep from brushing the crags with his wingtips, towered three times as high as the plane.

The landings at Skardu and Gilgit were also among the most dismaying experiences I have ever had in the air, and that includes plenty of bad storms, mountain flying at night with the radar gear broken, and a couple of minor crashes, not to mention combat flying in the Pacific war and a foolish night patrol to the Yalu over Red antiaircraft fire, the time I took part of my home leave in Korea.

At both Skardu and Gilgit, the unpaved strip was in a tiny valley hemmed around by some of the highest mountains in the world. In each case the gorge opened into the valley at an angle to the runway, so the pilot had to make a quick turn, let down over a boulder-strewn river bed, and then get his wheels on the ground fast, because the runway was just long enough. Coming out, the maneuvers were reversed: off the ground quick, over the rocks, wheel sharply, and dart into the gorge.

The Poles did this every day and seemed to think nothing of it. And I never heard of an accident on this most hazardous of all airplane routes.

Gilgit had had its own local revolution when the Maharajah's accession to India was announced. The Indian governor was taken prisoner by the Gilgit Scouts, the provincial military force, and from that point onward the area was administered by a Pakistani Political Agent sent from Karachi. The Gilgit district, while a part of Kashmir state, is one geographically, ethnically, and culturally with northern Pakistan, and the sentiment of the population, practically 100 per cent Moslem, is entirely for the Moslem Dominion. It has puzzled many observers how India could hope to hold this wild, distant, and hostile area in subjection.

Much of the Kashmir war, which lasted fourteen months, was fought in snow-blanked mountain passes, with both sides holding picket lines as high as 13,000 feet. It is said that no other war in history was ever waged at such heights.

India made free use of her air force against the foe, but Nehru warned that if Pakistan employed planes the Indians would not hesitate to carry bombing and strafing missions into Pakistani territory. That would no doubt have meant an all-out war between the two countries. Karachi was anxious to keep the action localized, so the impatient Pakistani pilots were restrained.

Between the Indians and the Pakistanis personally, it was a gallantly fought war. Until the partition in August 1947, the officers and men of the two armies had been comrades in arms and friends. Both sides were still using the same codes and procedures, which were thoroughly known to everybody. And both armies, at that time, owed nominal allegiance to the same King in London. The commander in chief on both sides was a British general and there were still many British officers and technicians in the Indian and Pakistani forces, but it was agreed that these should stay clear of the actual fighting zone. Had India and Pakistan resorted to formal, declared war, it was understood that all the British would be withdrawn.

Sometimes the personal friendliness that persisted between many Indian and Pakistani officers and enlisted men asserted itself in operations. It was related, for example, that an Indian unit once asked for and got Pakistani cooperation in an urgent communications matter. The Indians, it seems, were trying to transmit a wireless message and the Pakistanis, using the same frequency, kept interrupting. Finally an Indian officer, exasperated, got on the air.

"I say, you chaps," he addressed the Pakistanis in Oxonian English, "get off the bloody line, will you? I have a priority message here."

"Oh, righto, quite," a Pakistani, who may also have been

to Sandhurst, replied promptly. "Do carry on, old boy."

Then there was the Indian picket assigned to an active sector, who saw no sense in the daily waste of ammunition in impotent exchange of rifle fire across his observation post. Besides, he reasoned, it was dangerous.

So every morning, on taking his station, the Indian picket would shout a greeting to the Pakistani lines in Hindustani, the *lingua franca* of the armed forces.

"This is your friend, Sobha Singh!" he would call out. "I am here until evening, so let us have no shooting today!" And the rifles would remain silent.

Both sides may claim creditable showings in the Kashmir fighting. The Pakistanis scored several important victories, though handicapped by the injunction against air support. However, at the time the United Nations Commission for India and Pakistan obtained a ceasefire agreement, which became effective January 1, 1949, the Indians appeared about to take the last narrow sliver of territory held by Pakistan at the western end of the state's southern half. Nehru's agreement to the ceasefire, which left Pakistan holding that strip and the northern mountainous half of the state, was an unpopular move with the Indian Army, which had to stop fighting with victory apparently in its grasp.

The handling of the Kashmir issue in the United Nations Security Council was far from Nehru's expectations when he first took the case to that body, with a charge of aggression against Pakistan. The Council took little note of Nehru's accusations, but fastened instead upon his pledge to the people of Kashmir that the future of the state should be decided ultimately according to their wishes.

The Security Council interpreted Nehru's offer as meaning that a free plebiscite should be held when order was restored. There is room to doubt that Nehru meant any such thing. However, he could not with good grace refuse to accept the U.N. special commission's recommendation that a plebiscite be held with neutral United Nations supervision, under an administrator nominated by the Security Council but appointed formally by the government of Jammu and Kashmir. Fleet Admiral Chester W. Nimitz, U.S. Naval Commander in the Pacific in World War II, was named for the post and prepared to leave for Kashmir as soon as conditions could be agreed upon for the vote.

Nehru afterward indicated in several speeches that what he probably had in mind when he referred to ascertaining the "will of the people," was a vote on the accession by the Jammu and Kashmir Constituent Assembly as the "elected" representatives of the voting population.

This Assembly was voted into office in an election in which only two or three seats were contested. In all but these few unimportant instances, all candidates opposing the nominees of Sheikh Abdullah's National Conference party were somehow persuaded to withdraw. So in each district, with the exceptions noted, only one name appeared on the ballot. That left Srinagar with an Assembly representing only the National Conference, dominated by Sheikh Abdullah, who at that time passionately favored the Indian claims.

How did the people of Kashmir feel? Did they favor India or Pakistan? Well, it was not possible to take any kind of extensive private poll, but I never found any Kashmiri Moslem outside Sheikh Abdullah's circle who didn't state that he was wholeheartedly for Pakistan. I would estimate that 99 per cent of the foreign observers—newspapermen, diplomats, United Nations teams, tourists, and businessmen—who visited Kashmir, and to whom I talked in considerable numbers afterward, were convinced that in a fair plebiscite an overwhelming majority of Kashmiris would vote for Pakistan. The same opinion was also held by many Indians.

Plenty of Indians, officials and others, were heartily sick of the Kashmir dispute, without whose settlement there could never be satisfactory relations with Pakistan. Possibly a large majority of Indians, particularly in the distant south, cared nothing whatever about Kashmir except to the extent that they might be inclined patriotically to take the side of India in the quarrel with Pakistan. But Nehru cared, and that is what counted.

To me, there was never a visible possibility that a plebiscite such as the United Nations commission envisaged would ever be held.

I held this conviction because it was plain that Nehru's position, as he repeatedly stated it, could never be reconciled with Pakistan's conditions.

In the first place, Nehru contended that sovereignty over all Kashmir rested solely with India, and that the only legal government of the entire state, including the territory administered by the pro-Pakistani Azad Kashmir regime at Mirpur, was the Indian-supported machinery in Srinagar. The Indian Prime Minister was not willing to concede Pakistan any rights whatsoever in respect to the conduct of the proposed plebiscite.

The U.N. commission's protracted negotiations with India and Pakistan on conditions for the plebiscite finally broke down on the question of what military forces India could keep within the state while the voting was in progress. Nehru insisted that the security of Kashmir was entirely India's concern and responsibility. His final position was that India must maintain a minimum of 28,000 troops on her side of the ceasefire line, while in the sector held by Pakistan there might be a locally raised security force of four thousand, of whom only half should be recruited from pro-Pakistani elements. When Karachi found it impossible to agree to this ratio, efforts to settle the dispute through the United Nations ceased.

I once asked the late Sir N. Gopalaswami Ayyangar, long India's U.N. spokesman for the Kashmir case, "Why did India get into this plebiscite business, when technically it wasn't necessary?"

The old Brahmin smiled. "We hadn't had much experience then," he murmured.

Like all international tourist resorts, Kashmir derives a great deal of profit from traveling Americans, who flock to the well-advertised Vale in large numbers. It is characteristic of Americans to take some interest in what is going on around them wherever they happen to be. Though every newspaper reader in the United States must be aware that there is a "Kashmir question," few tourists seem to have any real knowledge of the issues when they arrive in New Delhi. When they finally arrive in Srinagar, their interest has been awakened and they begin asking questions. Soon discovering that the possibilities of agreement between India and Pakistan are remote, the natural reaction of the average tourist is to ask, "Why don't you make Kashmir independent, then? Hell, it's lots bigger than many independent countries."

From this a myth has grown in India that the United States is intriguing to cut Kashmir off from India and make it an independent state, where we could put military bases to threaten Russia and dominate all South Asia. This is a preposterous suggestion, because Kashmir is separated from Russia by some of the most impassable mountain barriers in the world, and this rugged country is not the kind one would mark out for a major air establishment in any case. The only interest, that I know of, that the American Embassy at New Delhi takes in Kashmir is to keep the State Department routinely informed of developments there.

Nevertheless, allegations of United States interference in Kashmir became so strong in the spring of 1954 that Ambassador George V. Allen put a ban on embassy personnel going to Srinagar for summer vacations, as had been a practice. Anti-American propaganda, enthusiastically promoted by the Communist party of India, reached its peak after the visit to Kashmir by Adlai Stevenson. The former Democratic Presidential candidate was alleged seriously to have conveyed an offer to Sheikh Abdullah from Washington of fifty million dollars in economic aid if Kashmir became independent!

But there was considerable substance in rumors of an independence movement in Kashmir, though Americans had nothing to do with it. I wrote, in the summer of 1948, in *The New York Times* that an officer of Sheikh Abdullah's government was talking to foreign correspondents, cautiously and vaguely, on the independence theme even then.

Although Sheikh Abdullah had faithfully supported India's case with all his considerable oratorical resources from the beginning, it was clear that the tall former schoolmaster was never too easy in his mind about leading the Moslems of Kashmir into an India ruled by Hindus. The actions of the extremist Hindus kept the Sheikh's doubts alive.

I recall a press conference called by the Sheikh early in 1950, at the time of the Hindu-Moslem outbreak in East and West Bengal—an episode so serious that again there was war talk in the air. After the newspapermen had finished questioning the Sheikh on Kashmir affairs, he said, "Now I'd like to ask you a few questions. When Hindus are slaughtering Moslems in West Bengal—and it is no excuse to say that Moslems are killing Hindus in East Bengal—how am I to tell my Kashmiri Moslems that they should join India? They come to me with this question. How do I justify it?"

This raised a clamor among the Hindu newspapermen, who are inclined to quick, passionate argument in defense of their rather strong feelings on most subjects. One of them, seeing that I had taken a note on the Sheikh's significant question, rose and said, with a glance at me, "This is off the record, of course, isn't it?" The Sheikh agreed to that, and when I arrived back at my hotel, quite a long time later, one of the Sheikh's secretaries was waiting for me to make sure I wasn't going to cable the observations about Hindus and Moslems.

The Sheikh's feelings on the subject have since landed him in jail.

The Hindus of Jammu province, dissatisfied with their poor economic condition while the Sheikh was carrying out highly publicized land reforms and other reform measures in the Vale, began to agitate against the Abdullah government, and by inference against Moslem rule, at the inspiration of an extremist Hindu political party called the Praja Parishad (people's party). Nehru warned that this sort of communal activity would have a bad effect on India's relations with Kashmir. The Prime Minister went unheeded by the fanatical Hindu, and there were anti-Abdullah demonstrations in Jammu wherein a number of persons were killed and some hundreds placed under political arrest.

Nehru was never more right in his apprehensions. Up until that time no Kashmiri dared speak publicly in favor of Pakistan's claims. Sheikh Abdullah was running a tight police state, and the jails did not lack clientele. Surveillance was quite rigid, as Jean and I had occasion to observe when we stayed a month in a houseboat.

Officials had denied, with a great show of hurt feelings, that the Sheikh's police were keeping a watch on visitors, or exercising any check on freedom of speech. However, as soon as we were installed in our houseboat a small cargo craft, the kind called a "country" boat with a thatched superstructure, tied up to the bank across from us. Men from this boat would question our servants, when we were absent, as to who our visitors had been, what we had talked about, and so on, so we knew they were police. After that I made it a daily practice to come out on deck every morning with a pair of immense field glasses and elaborately scan the police boat, the hills, everything about. Each time there would be a great flurry in the small boat, and after a few minutes one of the men would pedal off furiously on his bicycle, toward the police station.

I mentioned this to the government information secretary. He was skeptical, or pretended so, and promised to investigate. The next day he called and informed me that the police boat was there to watch not us but a nearby "houseboat of ill-repute."

If the vessel pointed out by the official was indeed a

"houseboat of ill-repute," it certainly wasn't doing much business. And the morning we left our floating abode to return to New Delhi, the police boat also shoved off.

There was a sudden surprising change with the rise of anti-Abdullah agitation in Jammu. All at once, anti-Indian voices began to be heard in Kashmir. Sheikh Abdullah began to make speeches in an unaccustomed nationalistic tone, in which it was easy to read a new mood, favoring an independent status for the state.

One Sunday morning in the dark hour before dawn, police walked in the door of Sheikh Abdullah's residence in Srinagar, announced that he was under arrest, and hustled him off to imprisonment in an old castle in another town. The Indian official radio that morning told the world that the Sheikh's government had been supplanted by a new regime headed by Bakshi Ghulam Mohammed, who had been the Sheikh's deputy prime minister. India at once disavowed any part or prior knowledge of the coup, explaining that the shake-up was the result of differences between the Sheikh and other members of his cabinet, which had caused the administration to collapse.

The new prime minister, Bakshi Ghulam Mohammed, immediately launched a strident propaganda campaign against "American intrigue," possibly in an attempt to divert attention from the incarceration of the Sheikh, who, we had been assured by the Indians for years, was the idol of Kashmiri Moslems. He was the idol of some, certainly, for his arrest was followed by an uprising in Srinagar, which government forces quickly put down at a cost of about a dozen lives of pro-Abdullah demonstrators.

There was a disposition in New Delhi to believe that Nehru, at least, had kept personally clear of the Bakshi coup. It is easy to imagine that his years of close friendship for Abdullah would not permit him to assist actively in the strong measures taken against his former trusted lieutenant. It is thought more likely that he turned the whole problem over to the late cabinet minister and trouble-shooter, Rafi Ahmed Kidwai, with carte blanche to handle the matter in his own way. Kidwai visited Kashmir just before the turn-over.

As time goes on and the Kashmir problem appears no nearer settlement, the suggestion is heard more and more both in India and Pakistan that the only solution possible is a partition of the state, based more or less on the current military disposition, and perhaps with a plebiscite limited to the Vale.

The United Nations ceasefire line, now separating the Indian and Pakistani areas, leaves the western strip, Gilgit, and the northern areas on the Pakistan side. Besides the Vale, India holds Jammu, which now is a Hindu majority area, and most of the eastern province of Ladakh, where the population is predominantly Buddhist, under the spiritual hegemony of the Dalai Lama of Tibet. On the basis of geography, ethnology, and religion, Pakistan has no more claim on Ladakh than India has on Gilgit, unless Pakistan also possesses Srinagar and the Vale.

While Jammu and Ladakh would certainly favor India in a plebiscite, and the western and northern areas would be solidly for Pakistan, there is room for a question as to how a referendum would go in the Vale. The pro-Indian elements have been in control here since the raiders were expelled in late 1947, and with many energetic rehabilitation projects under way, it would appear that the longer the plebiscite is postponed in the Vale the better India's chances will be. The one prediction I would venture is that there will never be a plebiscite in the state as a whole as long as Nehru is Prime Minister, unless it is certain that India will win.

9

A Confusion of Tongues

One day, while sitting in Lloyd's Bank waiting out the interminable process of cashing a check in an English countinghouse, I passed part of the time by examining closely an Indian one-rupee note. Apparently people don't look at one-rupee notes; maybe they don't have them long enough. For even Indians are invariably surprised when I tell them that this small bill contains the words "One Rupee" not only in nine different languages, but in *nine different scripts,* eight of them Indian. So far as I know, there is no other country in the world that prints its money in such a multiplicity of languages. But these nine, including English, are only the commonest. The Constitution of India recognizes fourteen major tongues for official national or provincial use. The 1951 census, an extraordinary mine of information on everything Indian, counts 720 languages and dialects.

In official life, English is still the *lingua franca* of India. Every Indian who has gone beyond elementary schooling can speak English. Of course, in a country where only 17 per cent of the population can read and write in any language, the number using English passably well is relatively very small. But when the total population is about three hundred and seventy million, it doesn't take a large percentage to make a tremendous number of people.

Wherever one goes in India, almost everyone with whom a foreigner would normally come in contact in his work, or in just getting around the country, speaks English of sorts. This excludes, broadly, the mass of unlettered peasants and laborers, the lowest ranks of police, office *peons* (messengers), and others in the bottom economic layer. Servants who have worked for British and Americans often speak English in varying degrees, although the British old-timers, unlike Americans, made it a point to know at least Hindustani, or the native tongue of the part of India they lived in.

"Indian English" has a distinct character often amusing to British and American ears. Indians tend to speak it, naturally, with the inflections and constructions peculiar to their native tongues; so it is possible to tell what part of India a man comes from by the way he speaks English, just as one can place an American by his regional accent. There is also a general use of archaic terms and constructions, called "babuisms" from the *babu* or clerk (pronounced clark) who uses them. These are probably heritages from the earliest days of the British who introduced their language in India, for it is a common saying that Indians still speak "Macaulay's English."

The highly educated classes, who speak English best, tend to do so with an accent more British than the British use. These professional men, service officers, officials, and businessmen often habitually speak English not only to foreigners but also among themselves and even in their families. It has often seemed strange to me to notice a table of Indians in a restaurant, with no foreigners among them, speaking nothing but English. For some of these, and I believe they include Nehru, English has actually supplanted the mother tongue (it is said that Nehru dreams in English; he told me himself once that his Hindi is not good, but I have heard others say that it is improving as he uses it more in his innumerable speeches around the country). A great many English-speaking Indians are truly bilingual, slipping from their native language into English and back again, often in the same sentence, so easily that I sometimes am convinced that they don't realize they are doing it.

Anglo-Indians, the mixed bloods, claim English as their mother tongue and almost invariably speak it with such an exaggerated Oxonian accent, and excessive sprinkling of English slang, that it has come to be a distinct accent of its own. When it is impossible to detect an Anglo-Indian by the color of his skin, either because his complexion is too light or too dark, he may betray his mixed race by the overcultivation of his English speech.

The Eurasian has found himself belonging to an unfortunate and suspected minority in all the Eastern countries that have been freed from foreign rule.

In the days of colonial rule, the Eurasian, generally speaking, tried to identify himself with the conquering race and to obscure his Asian background. Most mixed bloods being the product of unions between foreign men and local women, the Eurasian was usually set apart at once by his foreign surname. And color prejudice being by no means limited to the Caucasian race, he often suffered social discrimination at the hands of his darker cousins. So he turned to his Caucasian connections for whatever advantages they could bring him.

Under the British colonial government, there were distinct advantages in being an Anglo-Indian. They were trusted by the British—because they were not accepted by the Indians—and had almost a monopoly on key jobs in certain industries, particularly those important to British military security, such as the railroads and communications. An Anglo-Indian was practically assured of employment in these fields where, all other things being equal, the British would prefer an openly pro-British half-caste to an Indian of doubtful loyalty in a responsible position.

Precisely the same conditions that favored the Anglo-Indians under British rule became severe disadvantages when India was freed. Far from enjoying a preference in the services for which they had been trained, they became the objects of suspicion and discrimination. After independence, a further penalty of their former preferred status quickly became apparent. Being assured of a job in the railroads, telegraphs, and so on, the average young Anglo-Indian lacked the burning urge of his Indian cousin to improve his qualifications through higher study and determined exercise of his ambitions, as was necessary in the Indian's case. Consequently, with jobs on a purely competitive basis, the Anglo-Indian candidate, no longer at an advantage because of his British blood, was no match for his sharper and better educated Indian rival.

Consequently the Anglo-Indians today, numbering perhaps half a million, are in an unhappy situation as a community, being almost a "depressed class."

I have found Indians extraordinarily race conscious. "Racial equality" throughout the world is one of the cardinal principles of Indian foreign policy, yet color distinction is pronounced and open in India itself. This is partly because of the caste system, which has no counterpart elsewhere. Some authorities believe caste originated as a "color bar," one reason for this belief being that the Sanskrit word for caste and for color are the same, *varna.* But one sees color consciousness for its own sake every day in the newspaper matrimonial advertisements, which more often than not specify that the mate desired must be "fair-skinned." Preoccupation with fair skins in seeking marriage partners has become so much a part of the national life that Chakravarty Rajagopalachari, the famous elder statesman and scholar, once suggested publicly as an antidote that every light-skinned boy should marry a dark-skinned girl!

Apart from caste, pride of ancestry and culture is a marked characteristic of the Indian nation. In fact, the many different cultures are so strong individually that some authorities have questioned whether India can be considered a nation at all, but rather a congress of nations, like Europe. This point can be raised technically, but in practice the numerous disparate races of India have always possessed certain common approaches and outlooks. From these have grown a common patriotism for India as a country.

Nevertheless, provincialism and pride in one's particular clan and language remains an unsettling influence that leading Indians recognize and try to fight. A Bengali, for example, may think of himself as an Indian in relation to the rest of the world, but in relation to other Indians he is likely to think of himself first as a Bengali and only secondarily as a fellow citizen of India.

When one gets on an airplane in Delhi and travels in any direction, at the plane's first stop one may find oneself among people of a different language, different dress, different diet, in some instances a different race.

In an effort to level the linguistic barriers, at least, and also in the post-independence flush of nationalism, Hindi was adopted as the official language of India. This Sanskritized tongue, written in neat Devanagari script, is understood in some form by about half the population, far more than any other. But Hindi was, and still is, strongly opposed by many South Indians who refer to what they call "Hindi imperialism" as the symbol of political and economic pressures from the north, where Hindi is the mother tongue. In the South, where the principal regional languages have a Dravidian base, Sanskrit-based Hindi is as foreign as German, and they would have preferred English, which is better known than Hindi in this area of relatively high education. Nehru, who usually makes his public addresses in Hindi as a matter of policy more than preference, finds it expedient to speak in English before southern audiences, for then at least some will understand him.

Actually, Nehru's mother tongue is Urdu, the "camp language"—the word Urdu means "camp"—developed by the Mogul invaders and since brought to a high degree of beauty and expressiveness. But for a national language Nehru had gone along with Gandhi, who favored Hindustani, a sort of combination of Urdu and Hindi, written in either script. The term Hindustani has virtually gone out of use in India today, Hindi being substituted. Actually, true Hindi is highly classical and only sketchily understood by most of those who profess to speak it. The language used by the masses in the north and elsewhere, and the one that is learned by foreigners as "Hindi," is really Hindustani.

The promotion of true Hindi has had a strong Hindu religious force behind it, for it is close to Sanskrit, the language of the scriptures. The attitude of Hindi bigots was offensive to Moslems, which was the reason Gandhi and Nehru urged Hindustani. But the Hindi advocates, being the most powerful politically within the Congress party, won the day. Nehru now gives the impression that he is a Hindi proponent; when the Prime Minister suffers a defeat, as occasionally happens behind the scenes, he invariably appears afterward with the majority, apparently on the premise that "if you can't beat 'em, join 'em."

Hindi fanatics have classicized the language to an extreme, throwing out all the borrowed words from Urdu and other languages, and substituting fantastic circumlocutions from Sanskrit. When a synonym for an English or Urdu term does not exist in Sanskrit—because the idea to be expressed did not exist at the time Sanskrit was a spoken language—the meaning can only be conveyed by a definition. Thus, "radio" is translated into something like "celestial voice."

The expulsion of non-Sanskrit words from Hindi has made the language, particularly as used on the Hindi-conscious government radio and in staunch Hindi newspapers, largely incomprehensible to the man in the street. In some northern cities including Nehru's home town of Allahabad, where the strong Hindi advocates have got hold of the government, all the road signs, name boards, and so on that were in English have been replaced by translations into the classic tongue. Once Nehru, on his return to New Delhi from a visit to

Allahabad, complained publicly that his home town appeared to have adopted a new, strange language that he couldn't understand.

But in the common spoken language everywhere, many English words and technical terms are still used. In any garage in India, for example, a monkey wrench is "monkey wrench" no matter whether the mechanic is speaking Hindi, Marathi, Telegu, Tamil, or one of the other many tongues.

While Hindi is the national language, under the Constitution English will remain an official medium at least until 1965, by which year it is contemplated that Hindi will have gained sufficient currency to take over completely in courts, the Parliament, and elsewhere, where English is still largely employed. Probably more than 90 per cent of the voluminous utterances heard in India's garrulous Parliament are in English, for that is the only language most of the members have in common. There are a few illiterates in Parliament who understand only their provincial mother tongues, and consequently never know what is going on. There was one representative from an obscure aboriginal tribe who could understand only himself.

The total abolition of English does not meet favor with educators, who are appalled by the prospect of translating technical works into Hindi. But since English will continue to be a required study in the upper grades, it may well develop that English will also be retained as the language of higher instruction in the universities, at least in technical subjects. Meanwhile, the standard of English in India is constantly and noticeably declining, a matter on which many Indians, including Nehru, have remarked with regret.

There is now a movement in progress to simplify the writing of Hindi, so that the national language may be learned more quickly in the non-Hindi areas, and more conveniently adapted to printing machines. At the same time, the provincial languages have had to be conceded an official status for local purposes. Lower schools and courts, for instance, will continue to employ the mother tongue of the villagers exclusively, and it will be used also in the processes of municipal, district, and state administration. But in central government service all employees, at least above a certain level, will be required to know Hindi.

An Indian who does not originate in one of the Hindi-speaking northern states and who aspires to the civil service now will have to know at least three languages. He will be naturally equipped with his mother tongue, and will have to keep expert in its use if he is brought up in his home state; he will have to be fluent in Hindi to enter the government employ; and he will still, let us face it, have to be proficient in English if he wants to equip himself for aspiration to the top levels.

Pride in provincial languages has contributed immensely to what Indians call "fissiparous tendencies," to use a good example of a "babuism." Many of the leading languages possess an ancient and honored literature, and are spoken in daily life by greater numbers of people than are embraced by many European languages. For example, the thirteen million speakers of Malayalam, one of the most obscure of the major Indian tongues, are almost as numerous as the users of all the Scandinavian languages together.

Hindi, in its several forms, follows Chinese and English as the third most used language in the world. Telegu, Tamil, Marathi, Punjabi, and Gujerati, among others, will be found high in any extensive numerical listing of principal languages rated according to the number of users.

Adherents of the various languages have agitated many years for a recasting of the Indian provinces along linguistic boundaries, somewhat on the pattern of the Soviet linguistic republics. The Indian National Congress, interested in uniting opinion against British rule, endorsed this movement on the grounds that the British provincial borders were arbitrary and often accidental. The Congress linguistic platform became an embarrassment suddenly when that revolutionary organization became overnight the governing party of free India.

It is seen now that while some revision in the grouping of states may be desirable, a complete capitulation to sectional ambitions is neither politically wise nor entirely practical. On the other hand, some concession to linguistic nationalism would end, or at least reduce, one important source of local agitation against the government that the Communists and others have exploited with some success.

Many considerations were placed before a nonpartisan commission appointed to study the problem over a period of several years. For one, nothing must be done to encourage linguistic nationalism so as to damage the unity of the new Indian nation. Secondly, a regrouping on purely linguistic lines would disturb the economic order to an appreciable extent, as some of the new states thus created would be in perpetual financial difficulties, for they would face a chronic deficit in food crops and other revenue-producing enterprises.

There would be the problem also of multilingual cities, notably Bombay and Madras, where rival linguistic groups push their claims with bitter energy. The eventual decisions are likely to have a profound influence on the future unity of India as a state, producing either a greater homogeneity of interest than has ever existed before, or adding to the elements that might contribute to an ultimate breakup, as has been the pattern of Indian history through past ages.

For these reasons the redisposition of the states may be the most important project taken in hand by the government, outside the economic sphere, since independence.

10

Panditji

FOR THOUSANDS OF YEARS, THE PATTERN OF HISTORY IN INDIA has been one of rebellion, secession, and conquest. The Empire of Asoka, two centuries before Christ; the peak of the Mogul rule; then the British Raj—these were the three periods when centralized power reached its high points. In between, there was a continuing process of change, of empires rising and falling. The establishment of India and Pakistan as independent, democratic states in 1947 offered for the first time a prospect of permanence. The relations between East and West Pakistan, separated by a thousand miles of Indian territory and split politically and emotionally on numerous issues, leave room for doubt that this difficult arrangement will endure. But the present Republic of India shows far greater stability and promise of continued unity than the subcontinent has ever seen before. It is possible that under the stress of a great calamity, such as a defeat in war, India might again break apart, but meanwhile the strength of the Indian Union continues to grow.

The diversion of the erratic course of Indian history has been largely the work of three men: Mohandas Karamchand Gandhi, Vallabhbhai Patel, and Jawaharlal Nehru. These were the titans of the independence movement that ultimately achieved its goal in 1947.

At this point Gandhi retired more or less to the role of elder statesman, his life's work done, and was soon to die by an assassin's bullet. Patel, until his death several years later, guided the consolidation of the new country, eliminating the princes and implementing the powers of the central government in New Delhi. With the passing of Patel, Nehru alone carries the burden of welding the disparate and contentious peoples of India into a unified nation.

Nehru is peculiarly well equipped to lead the transformation of India, almost overnight in terms of historic time, from a backward, feudal condition into the company of progressive twentieth-century states. The challenge of his task is perhaps best summed up in his own remark that "India has to run before she has learned to walk."

Asia was passed over by the Industrial Revolution to which Europe and America can trace their present advancement. The revolution of political thought that also transformed the West in the eighteenth and nineteenth centuries was not permitted to take hold in Asia, which in that period was coming under Western colonial dominance. So when India's fetters were stricken in 1947, she had to install in a moment what other countries had evolved slowly, over a long period. It was a simple matter to state economic and social goals, but their achievement rested on the capability of the Indian people to overcome an endless background of repression, attended by enforced economic and political innocence.

Fortunately, many Indians individually had already bridged the gap mentally between yesterday and tomorrow. The British, almost from the beginning, had trained Indians to man the various services, and it reflects favorably on both the Indians and the British that Britain was able to rule India so long with only a handful of imported officials.

Long before 1947, Indians were ready to take over the civil service, said to be the best in the world; the courts, educational system, and all the other paraphernalia of administration that had been instituted on British lines.

It required no adjustment either to assume full responsibility for defense, the railroads and telegraphs (which had been started nearly one hundred years before), and the rest of the country's physical plant. But the normal nationalist disposition to throw out the British lock, stock, and barrel was curbed, and a number of advisors were kept on in Indian pay to assist the transfer of the higher echelon positions that the British had retained for themselves.

Nehru, as much as any Indian, was a product of Britain and India together. He has described himself as "a man of two worlds, at home nowhere." But in leading India from darkness into light, his dual background was an advantage. He had been brought up in the polished, Westernized circles revolving around the Allahabad home of his father, Pandit Motilal Nehru, a wealthy lawyer and an Indian nationalist who admired the British and remained on good terms with them even when jailed. It is said that during the periods of Motilal Nehru's incarceration he was accustomed to entertaining high-ranking British officers and officials with champagne in his cell.

His boyhood in Motilal Nehru's house accustomed the young Jawaharlal to moving in sophisticated, cosmopolitan circles. It was luxurious surrounding, rather far removed from the life of the masses of India whom Jawaharlal was to know so well in later years. Motilal Nehru was a high-liver, from all accounts, who regularly sent his laundry to Paris. Young Jawaharlal had an English governess, who, it is said, trained the boy to look upon Americans as generally uncouth specimens with atrocious speech and inadmissible table manners by calling his attention to solecisms and gaucheries as she regarded them, committed by American visitors to his father's house.

At Harrow and Cambridge, young Nehru was a fashionable youth, but on his return to India, with the education of a barrister like his father, he entered into the independence movement as a disciple of Gandhi. By 1929, he rose to the presidency of the Indian National Congress, a position he was to hold five times. After the deaths of Gandhi and Patel,

Nehru was able to exercise unchallengeable control over the Congress party; in various serious disputes on Congress policy he forced the adoption of his own point of view by simply threatening to resign if he didn't get his way. Few Indians can conceive of dispensing with Nehru's services as Prime Minister and party leader, and it is largely through his personality that Congress is able to maintain its hold on the country.

At once an aristocrat, a Socialist, and an agnostic, Nehru was an odd partner to the ascetic, religious Gandhi. They often disagreed, but Nehru submerged his personal convictions before disagreements ever approached the point of open breach, because he was above all convinced that the freedom struggle would succeed only through the unity of the country behind the Congress program, which in turn owed its vitality to Gandhi's leadership. Later, he was to come in conflict with Patel, the political boss of the party, who did not always accept Nehru's idealistic disregard of the demands of practical politics. Again, Nehru recognized his need of the other man, and, on the whole, they formed a balanced team.

Even after independence had been achieved, the united front of the Congress high command was never permitted to show its internal flaws before the public. An instance was the contest for the first Presidency of the Indian Republic. Nehru was known to favor Chakravarty Rajagopalachari, who was then Governor-General, the first Indian to hold this position. "Rajaji," besides being a wise older counselor whom Nehru wished to retain in the capital, was a great favorite with foreign diplomats and an able ceremonial representative of his country. Patel and the powerful Hindu element of Uttar Pradesh, Bihar, and other states of the north were backing Rajendra Prasad, another "elder statesman" and a Gandhian of great influence and renown. The President was to be elected by the Constituent Assembly, forerunner of the present Parliament. Rivalries between northern and southern factions came into play, and a first-class political joust was building up. But it was considered damaging to the position of Congress before the country to allow the issue to come to a vote. When it appeared that, if there were a vote, Prasad was bound to win, Rajagopalachari stepped out and, as far as the public record shows, Nehru concurred wholeheartedly in the selection of Prasad.

Nehru is not noted in India as either an administrator or a politician. As the executive head of the government, he has perhaps a better grasp than any other individual of the nature and needs of the country, and he puts forth many attractive ideas. His weakness lies in implementation; he appears to be incapable of putting his suggestions into effect at the administrative level with the ruthless force of the late Sardar Patel. He shows dictatorial tendencies, without a dictator's strength.

And his hold on the Congress political machine, which he must control in order to put through his legislative program, appears to rest solely on the party's need of him as the unquestioned idol of the voters. The many powerful opponents of Nehru in Congress party councils realize that if he were to leave them and form another party of his own, they would quickly be voted out of their seats of influence.

The subservience of the party's high command to Nehru's personality was most strikingly proved when he forced the retirement of Purshottamdas Tandon, leader of the Hindu extremist faction, as party president and stood successfully for the office himself. Nehru has said that he preferred that the functions of Prime Minister and Congress president be separated, but when party policy under Tandon began to head in directions Nehru opposed, he stepped in and seized the reins without hesitation.

If the Congress party's strength lies to a great extent in Nehru, the Prime Minister conceives that the strength of the party is the strength of the country. There is no doubt, as Nehru has admitted, that Congress has failed to keep touch with the masses of the people and has lost in the confidence of the electorate since independence. But he insists that Congress is the only party with an organization effective enough to carry on an administration.

As a lifelong member of the party and often its president, Nehru's loyalty is deep. He would leave the Congress only if he were convinced that the party's policies were leading the country into objectionable paths, and that could not happen so long as Nehru maintained his present control.

Nehru is the first to admit that he is not a skillful politician. Patel was, and his passing left a heavy and unwelcome burden on Nehru as the arbiter of party affairs. Once, when Nehru was put up for the Congress presidency some years ago before independence, an unsigned article appeared in leading Indian newspapers denouncing him as a willful person with possible aspirations to become a dictator. The anonymous analysis was the most penetrating and unflattering critique of Nehru ever published to that time. There was immediately an indignant outcry against this unknown detractor. It then leaked out that Nehru had written the article himself, in the hope that it would distract his supporters for an office he did not happen to want at that time!

After Gandhi, Nehru's hold on the masses of India is unparalleled. In his numerous trips about the country, it is not unusual for him to draw crowds counted in hundreds of thousands. Many of his listeners, outside the Hindi-speaking areas, may have little or no idea what he is saying, but they will travel miles to see him. Many times I have seen villagers sit for an hour or more as if spellbound, their eyes riveted on his face in an unmoving stare, as he discoursed to them in a language of which they understood not a word. A lot of this devotion is traceable, no doubt, to the Hindu concept of *darshan*, the spiritual benefit that Hindus believe they gain by sharing the presence of a great or saintly person.

Nehru draws a kind of *darshan* in reverse from the immense crowds he addresses. From what he has said of this, he appears to believe that some mystic exchange takes place between himself and a great concourse of people, by which he comes to know the mind of his country. This is true in a sense, but one is not sure it is so because Nehru gives the people what they want, or because the people discover a want for what he gives them. However, the effect is the same in either case, and there is no doubt that when Nehru speaks he voices the overwhelming opinion of India.

His personal contacts with villagers and other representatives of the masses are by no means confined to the lecture platform. Within the limits of his time he seizes every opportunity to exchange views with the common man, and he is as accessible as it is possible for him to be.

Nehru's program of speeches and travel on a typical tour, often over rough and dusty roads and in extreme heat, has often taxed the physical powers of the younger men who accompany him. Nehru at sixty-five is a robust specimen, with no experience of illness in the years I have known him, beyond a routine cold or sore throat. He keeps his muscles in firm tone with exercises including his famous yogic practice of standing on his head for a few minutes each morning. He says that standing on his head gives him mental as well as physical relaxation, for "it is impossible to take the world seriously when you are looking at it upside down." And his trips, strenuous as they are, always leave him looking younger and refreshed.

Yet his heavy work schedule in New Delhi, which seldom leaves him more than four or five hours for sleep, often makes its mark upon his tawny face in deep, dark lines. His true vacations, entirely away from official demands, amount to no more than a few days a year, often spent in his beloved Kashmir. He is constantly adding complications to his already exacting routine by agreeing to address conferences of all sorts, lay cornerstones for civic buildings all over the country, hand out diplomas, and so on. He cut his social schedule drastically by decreeing that he would attend no more of the yearly "national day" receptions of the more than forty foreign missions in New Delhi, except India's own and those of the other British Commonwealth countries. He accepts a few private dinner invitations, and is called upon by his position to do a certain amount of quiet dinner entertaining himself. He often has guests to lunch, however, and sometimes even to breakfast. Incidentally, for himself he prefers Western food, and eats meat, as his particular Brahmin caste is nonvegetarian. And whether by preference or because of India's prohibition policy, he is never seen to partake of alcohol.

Nehru's moods, wherever he may be, are unpredictable. At formal press conferences he is invariably genial and witty. In recent years he has learned to handle such affairs urbanely and surely, and has done so in many countries before newspapermen of all nationalities. He has become a master of parrying delicate questions, often leaving the questioner unsure whether he has been answered or not.

Consciously or not, he has learned to check the famous flashes of anger that often enlivened his earlier press conferences. But he has by no means lost the volatility of temperament that shows in sudden bursts of irritation. Once he charged me, in some annoyance, with having written unfairly that he had a quick temper. "And I heard," I told him, "that when you read that you lost your temper." At this he laughed.

Individual contacts with press correspondents may be fortunate or not, depending upon the circumstances and the type of questions he is asked. Elementary and worn-out questions, like "what do you think of communism?" or "what is the aim of the five-year-plan?" often asked by newcomers to India are likely to leave him disgusted with the mentality of the interviewer, and it will be difficult to get a worthwhile statement out of him. He is especially sensitive to any question that smacks of a patronizing attitude, an offense of which many Americans—and not only correspondents—are often unwittingly guilty. But a penetrating question that intrigues Nehru, that strikes at the heart of an important matter, or that reveals a superior understanding on the part of the questioner, may bring forth a profound and interesting exposition of the Prime Minister's views at some length.

Visiting correspondents who succeed in obtaining an interview with Nehru—it isn't always easy—are usually received about seven o'clock in the evening in his second-floor sitting room, a fair-sized chamber decorated with a pair of immense, delicately carved elephant's tusks, and autographed photographs of various international statesmen and heads of government he has met. The windows look out on the spacious garden of the former residence of the British commander in chief, now the official home of India's Prime Minister. He lives in this huge, stately mansion with his daughter, Mrs. Indira Gandhi, her two children, and a corps of secretaries and typists who work the night through in the rooms allotted to office space. If the visitor happens to come in the daytime, he will probably be shown Nehru's two pet Himalayan pandas, presented to him by the hill tribes. At night, the conversation will be punctuated by the high-pitched, eerie howl of the jackals that prowl the dimly lit streets of New Delhi after dark.

It is not easy to make small talk with the Prime Minister, especially if he happens to be bored or preoccupied, with his mind far from his present surroundings. It is not unusual to see him standing alone at a large reception, gazing about with a dark frown; it is difficult to tell whether his mind is far away, on some problem, or whether he is reflecting on his immediate surroundings with distaste.

For Nehru is a patrician among Indians, a man of the highest birth in the world's oldest and tightest social hierarchy. He is a Kashmiri Brahmin, which is all that it is necessary to say in India to define his rarefied status in the Hindu society. The Brahmins are the topmost of the four caste levels, the traditional priests and scholars, and the Kashmiri Brahmins are the highest among these, for they have their roots in the Himalayas, the dwelling place of the gods. Their ancestors gained an immense respect, which has been passed down through succeeding generations, for having stood out against conversion to Islam when millions of other Hindus meekly bowed to the invader and changed faith.

Nehru himself scorns caste, and has forbidden the use of his title of Pandit, with which all Kashmiri Brahmins are born. Informally, however, his associates still call him "Panditji"—"ji" being a respectful suffix—and it is unlikely that he will ever be able to shake this reminder of his exalted caste status, for that is how he is referred to all over India.

No longer a Hindu by religion, if he ever was—he has called himself an agnostic—Nehru nevertheless cannot avoid his Hindu background, which makes him a member of a particular order of society, conditioned in certain patterns of thinking; nor can he revoke the Brahmin heritage that makes him an aristocrat of his race, however sternly he may discipline himself in the doctrine that all men are created equal. In spite of himself he is a patrician of patricians, and it would be surprising if he were not unconsciously a bit of a snob.

The Nehru family was originally named Kaul, a common Kashmiri Brahmin name. After migrating to Delhi long ago, the family dwelled by the side of a waterway and acquired the name Nehru, meaning "canal."

Like many others who are revolted by the present-day outward forms of Hinduism, Nehru admires and has absorbed the philosophic approach to life developed by great Indian thinkers over thousands of years. But he sometimes cannot repress his scorn for the superstitions and ceremonials that surround ordinary practice of the religion, as evidenced recently when he roughly shoved aside a Brahmin priest who attempted to involve him in an elaborate Hindu rite as he was dedicating a building.

The subservience of Hindus to prominent figures, like himself, never fails to enrage him. It is a custom of the Hindu to kneel and touch the feet of a great man, and when this occasionally happens to Nehru, on his travels in the country, the respectful gesture always sends him immediately into a towering fury. This, he says, is one of the things wrong with India. Others, like the devout and orthodox President Rajendra Prasad, do not share this rebellion against the mumbo jumbo of Eastern religions.

When Nehru suggested, in 1954, that it might be time he retired from the Prime Ministership, there were many skeptics who said he was merely exercising a familiar political trick to rally support in the country. But some of his associates were not so sure. They thought that here again his heritage might be asserting itself through the overlay of Westernism in Nehru's character, for he is now at about the age when the Brahmin traditionally retires to a life of contemplation. Some of those who know him best would not be surprised if some day Nehru did step down, although this time he withdrew his suggestion in the face of an enormous public outcry for him to stay.

11

After Nehru, Who?

Nehru is at his best among the people, and it is in his efforts, singlehanded, to mold the masses of India into a homogeneous nation that his greatest contribution to his country lies. Others can run the administration of government, overhaul the wobbling economy, and conduct foreign relations as well as Nehru, perhaps in many instances better. But Nehru is the one Indian who can grip the imagination of the people from Kashmir to Cape Comorin, and weld them into a national entity bent upon achieving a great destiny. This can be a lifelong task; it is questionable whether his inevitable successor will be able to wield the same magnetic influence upon millions who are often of a different race and cannot even understand his words.

With the possible exception of the Pope of the Roman Catholic Church, Nehru undoubtedly has the largest individual following of any man alive today. Probably few leaders in all history, besides Gandhi, could count so many sincere, admiring adherents.

In traveling the length and breadth of India and poking into many remote corners of the country as well as all the great cities, I have heard more criticism of Nehru than of any other figure in the government. That is natural, because it is an elected government answerable to the people, and Nehru is the head of it. In any country where there is free speech, the chief executive of the state must bear the brunt of dissatisfactions that are bound to exist on every side until Utopia is reached. Yet I never had the slightest doubt that an overwhelming majority of India's 370,000,000 people, even including the Communists, want Nehru to remain as their leader, and cannot imagine India without him. Some would make some changes in the way things are done, that is all.

A hardheaded Indian observer, one of Nehru's severest critics, once suggested to me that "if the Communists took over India, Jawaharlal Nehru would be their Prime Minister." I think there is something in that. If a Communist government came to power and Nehru were asked to head it, he might conceive it his duty to India to accept, if in doing so he were not required to make too great a compromise with his own principles. This would require important concessions on the part of the Communists, but certainly they would be willing to pay a heavy price for Nehru's name and leadership. At the moment, however, a Communist victory in India is a most unlikely hypothesis, and this is due in no small measure to Nehru's opposition to them.

One must see Nehru in action in the hustings to appreciate fully the magnitude of the task he has set himself, and the effect of his personality on scores of millions of his people.

I remember a night in Trivandrum, near the extreme southern tip of India, in Travancore-Cochin State. This was at the height of a state election campaign, in which the Communists were a strong contender to win. Nehru stood on a floodlighted platform, looking over a vast concourse of chocolate-brown bodies, the men half-naked in the heat of the still, tropic night. Moonlight turned the tall palm trees to silver, glinted on the gold and silver anklets and necklaces of the women, winked from the tiny diamonds in their noses. The crowd, about 200,000 including thousands who had come from far villages by bullock cart through the heat and dust, sat impassively, frozen-faced. Eyes glistening, they watched Nehru under the lights. The language here was

Malayalam, one of the Dravidian group bearing no relation to Hindi, so Nehru spoke in English. Only a small fraction of the audience could understand a word he said, but they sat through his hour-long speech and applauded wildly when he finished.

The next day I followed his motorcade to the Land's End of India, Cape Comorin, named after the temple of Kumari, the virgin aspect of Kali, the goddess of destruction, at the very southernmost tip of the great Indian peninsula.

I had been to this famous place of pilgrimage before, by the regular motor road down from Trivandrum. This time, following Nehru's open convertible American car, we detoured onto narrow, unpaved side roads, going deep into the jungle and down to the sea. We paused at several dozen villages, some of which were inhabited by Moslems descended from Arab sailors who sought the riches of the Malabar Coast more than a thousand years ago, perhaps even in the lifetime of the Prophet. Our passage was a triumphal procession through a series of welcoming arches, one at the entrance to each village, made of bamboo, palms, and flowers.

Here and there, all along the way, a Communist red flag flew from the top of a palm tree, but it looked like the entire population of every little settlement turned out to see Nehru, for the people were all by the roadside, none in the houses. At each stop Nehru made a short speech, and a dozen or more garlands of marigolds were draped about his neck. The police precautions were extreme, with barbed wire wherever the Prime Minister was to stop, but Nehru encouraged the crowds to gather close.

The Communists did not win that election.

Another time I followed Nehru through the wild Naga and Lushai Hills of far Assam, near the Burma border. Here he was among his most beloved tribesmen, the unspoiled hill people to whom he claims to belong from his origins in the mountains of Kashmir. The Nagas are of Mongolian race, and look much like American Indians, especially in their tribal costume of blankets and barbaric feather headdresses. Here again Nehru was an alien, even as I. As much as myself, he was of a different race, his native language was even less comprehensible to these tribespeople than English, which they were accustomed to hearing from missionaries and the former British officials; and his clothing, the *achkan* and *churidar* of a gentleman of quality from far-off Uttar Pradesh, was stranger to the tribal audience than my own khaki slacks and shirt.

In the craggy, cool Naga Hills and in the steamy humidity of tropical Travancore, Nehru followed a formula he has developed for awakening in all the peoples of India, hill tribesmen, coastal fishermen, and desert dwellers who know vaguely if at all of each other's existence, a sense of union.

He concluded each speech with the national slogan, "Jai Hind!" (long live India). Many of the tribes, particularly, may never have heard the Hindi words before.

Then he would raise his arms, and by a gesture understandable in any language, he would signal to the crowd to repeat the slogan with him. Three times he would bid the audience to join in, each time louder, like a college cheer leader. It was Nehru's way of instilling a consciousness that the tricolor flag of India covers all her children—the high-cheeked Mongols of the northern hills, the light-skinned Aryans like himself, the dark Dravidians of the perpetually sunny south, Hindus, Moslems, Christians, Jews, and totem-worshiping tribes.

As I watched these demonstrations, and heard Nehru explain to wild, untutored audiences the simple principles of patriotism and nationhood, as if he were reading from the most elementary of civics texts, I could not help feeling a wave of deep sympathy and admiration for this cultivated man, aristocrat and Brahmin, joint product of East and West, who stumps the jungles, the deserts, and the crags to bring to the disparate peoples of his vast country a new feeling of nationhood.

More than Nehru's political leadership and his guidance of diplomatic and economic policy, the masses of India from Kashmir to the Cape, from the burning Punjab to the jungled Burma border, will miss the unifying influence of his presence. Above a morass of incompetence, narrow sectional interest, and personal ambition, Nehru's voice rings clear and alone in the villages.

In the normal course of events, Nehru should be active for many years to come. His health is excellent; and while the average life-span in India is only thirty-two years, the leaders live to an extraordinarily active old age. It would set no precedent in India if Nehru were still in the government at eighty-five; there is at least one great political leader still going strong in the south who is older than that.

But who would succeed Nehru if he were to pass from the scene tomorrow? Although he has never appeared to be grooming a successor, which is an unusual thing among great national figures, there are candidates.

For political reasons, the exceptionally able men in the civil service are ruled out. For one thing, they have stayed aloof from politics, and the Congress party is likely to insist that the leader be one of its own. Secondly, it is too early to forget that the civil service was the organ through which the British ruled India; some of the outstanding officials who might possess qualifications to head the government even held British knighthoods for their services to the Crown.

In the Congress fold, a likely possibility seems to be Morarji Desai, now chief minister of Bombay State. Desai is a dedicated Gandhian of high intelligence, extreme capability, and long political experience. His integrity is unsurpassed, he has a countrywide reputation, and he is admired within the party. His weakness, though he would undoubtedly call it one of his strengths, is a fanatical devotion to Gandhi's prohibition movement.

Though Indians are not on the whole a bibulous race, there is a respectable percentage of drinkers, and the more sophisticated class in the Army, the services, government, and business are against prohibition on principle. Nevertheless, over considerable opposition Desai forced prohibition onto his state—under the administrative system it was not necessary to take a vote on the question, and no referendum has been held—and remained sternly oblivious to the fact that he took much of the life out of the great cosmopolitan city of Bombay, and caused an extensive illicit liquor business to spring into being with all its attendant evils. But with India going gradually dry anyway, Desai's prohibitionism may not be a factor in his chances to become Prime Minister.

Other names prominently mentioned are those of Dr. B. C. Roy, Gandhi's physician and chief minister of West Bengal; and Govind Ballabh Pant, now Home Minister and one of the most respected figures in the Congress, until recently chief minister of India's largest state, Uttar Pradesh. Against them is the fact that both these men are approaching seventy and ailing.

It was thought for a time that Nehru himself favored the youthful Socialist leader, Jayaprakash Narayan, and the idea was not unpopular.

Ideologically, Nehru himself is a Socialist, as are many Asians who do not subscribe to the doctrinaire platforms of the Socialist party. When the Indian Socialists formed a wing of the Congress party, Nehru and the younger man—Narayan has just turned fifty-two—had a sympathetic association. A couple of years ago Nehru proposed to Narayan a "working arrangement" between the Congress and the Socialists. This would have amounted to a voting coalition in Parliament and the state legislatures, but not a party merger.

Some political observers thought this move was intended

by Nehru as a prelude to bringing Narayan into the government, in the expectation that practical experience in the problems of governing would rub off certain doctrinaire beliefs that Nehru considers unworkable. Narayan agreed in principle to the coalition, but he presented a list of conditions that went right down the line of standard Socialist doctrine. He demanded Congress adherence to the Socialist platform, including nationalization of all industry without compensation, outright seizure of land for redistribution, and other policies that Nehru could not accept.

Shortly afterward Narayan announced his retirement from politics, but many Indians believe that the last has not been heard of this brilliant and attractive man, educated at the University of Wisconsin. Narayan has covered the entire country in his political activities, and has an enormous personal following among intellectuals, laborers, and peasants.

It is expectable that the passing of Nehru would be followed by a scramble for his office among powerful factions in the Congress party, with no candidate able to command a sufficient following to emerge as a clear-cut choice on which all could agree. In that case, a most likely one, an "elder statesman" like President Prasad, Rajagopalachari, or Pant might be designated to take over for an interim period until the party could be consolidated behind a younger man. In any case, India can be counted upon to produce some sagacious and capable figure to carry on, though it may not seem like the same India without Nehru's towering personality at the helm.

12

His Excellency

PERCY WOOD, *The Chicago Tribune* CORRESPONDENT, AND I were chatting with Sir Homi Mody, Governor of Uttar Pradesh State, in his ornate sitting room after lunch at his elaborate residence in Lucknow. Sir Homi was a rich Bombay financier, a member of the prosperous Parsi community, Zoroastrians who first came to India some twelve hundred years ago from Persia to escape Moslem persecution. Largely concentrated in Bombay, they worship in the Fire Temples before the eternal flame signifying the light and glory of God, and they leave their dead on top of the Towers of Silence to be devoured by vultures, thus returning life to life. The Parsis, numbering not more than 100,000, are the most progressive, enlightened and successful single religious community in India, and are noted for their philanthropies. Sir Homi Mody belongs to the group of great Parsi industrialists who produced the Tata enterprises, one of the top-ranking business empires in the world.

We were talking to Sir Homi, casually, about the curious (to us) institution of which he was a part, the system of "constitutional governors" of the Indian states. Whereas in the United States the governor is the chief executive, in India he has the same relationship to the state as the President has to the nation: he is more or less a figurehead, required to sign legislation but possessing no veto power, with no responsibilities but to open the state assembly and to appear on formal occasions. Like the President, he provides continuity in government and may be called upon to govern the state under emergency powers when there is no cabinet functioning. This is called "governor's rule," and is invoked only in time of disaster or when the administration threatens to break down under political stresses, as when no party or coalition of parties can rally sufficient support in the state legislature to keep a cabinet in office.

The Governor is addressed as "His Excellency," and lives in an atmosphere of pomp and ceremony usually associated only with reigning royalty, with aides-de-camp, hordes of servants in resplendent livery, and a palace to live in which used to be called "Government House" in British times, but has been changed by the Indians to "Raj Bhavan," which means the same thing. (The President's palace in New Delhi, formerly the residence of the Viceroys, similarly has been redesignated "Rashtrapati Bhavan.")

"How many servants do you suppose I have here?" said Sir Homi idly.

"Oh, perhaps a hundred," Percy replied, guessing.

Sir Homi laughed indulgently.

"Why, there are many more than that," he chuckled. We never did find out how many.

The governorship is an institution inherited from the British, like India's parliamentary form of government. The Prime Minister of the country, and the chief minister of a state, are the executives. They and their cabinets are formally appointed by the President, or governor in the case of a state, on their designation by the leading party in the national Parliament or state legislature, as the case may be. The cabinet, like that of the United Kingdom or France, lasts only so long as it can command a majority in the legislative body. A majority vote of "no confidence" brings the government crashing down, and if no stable alternate cabinet can be found there has to be a new election. The President, or governor in a state, either forms an interim or "caretaker" cabinet, or runs the government personally under his emergency powers until the balloting can be arranged.

The system has the advantage of making the administration continually responsible to the people's elected representatives, instead of being assured of office for a given period of years. The disadvantage is that a multiplicity of political parties may make it impossible for any one group to command a dependable majority in the legislative body for long, resulting in a continual turmoil.

This has happened in several Indian states since independence. But "His Excellency" is always there as a symbol of the permanence of the state, like a constitutional monarch or the President of France.

"But it's pretty expensive, this constitutional governor business," I suggested to Sir Homi Mody.

"Well, yes," he said, "but the people like it, you see. Indians have always been accustomed to pomp and show in their rulers, and they want it in their new government. It's part of their tradition and character."

The formal parties and ceremonial occasions at Rashtrapati Bhavan—which Clemenceau commented admiringly would make "a magnificent ruin"—are a colorful show, with a guard of tall Sikhs, in uniforms of scarlet and gold and mounted on magnificent horses, and carrying pikes. None of the panoply associated with the British Viceroys has been abandoned, although part of the immense red sandstone building, with its great dome and miles of corridors, has been converted into offices and a national museum.

Dr. Prasad, one of the simplest of human beings and the man in the Indian government most like Gandhi in his character and habits, protested at taking up residence in the viceregal palace. He asked to have one of the many cottages on the extensive grounds, where certain officials live. But Nehru insisted that the dignity of India required the President to dwell in suitable surroundings. Obediently but reluctantly, the honest old Gandhian moved in with his tiny, self-effacing wife, Rajbunchi, and his numerous relatives and grandchildren. But first the kitchens had to be purified of possible defilement by nonorthodox cooks. The President was the first high Indian official—and possibly the only one—to declare that his salary was too high in such a poor country and regularly to turn part of it back.

It was natural that India should continue British government forms, despite all the talk about "Indianizing" and the return to ancient culture, since virtually all that Indians know of modern ways in any field they observed through British eyes. Indians are accustomed to British ways and admire them. It is only occasionally, and usually when he has had a few drinks too many, that an Indian reveals lurking bitterness against the British for earlier humiliations and mistreatment. Apparently, to Indians, the good that the British left behind atoned for their "crimes."

Ironically, the British created a strength and community of outlook among Indian leaders that might otherwise be lacking and that stands the country in good stead today, by the very repressive measures used to try to break up the independence movement. Being in jail together, many times and for long periods, fused such clashing personalities as Gandhi, Nehru, and Patel into a common understanding that held them together later when disagreements might have been permitted to weaken their cause. Nehru, who spent thirteen years in jail altogether, still feels a deep personal bond of sympathy and understanding with some of the opposition leaders who criticize his policies in Parliament, because he was in prison with them, too. And as Nehru said himself, prison may have been of great personal benefit to him, for it gave him leisure to read, and think, and write his great books, which are the finest literature written by any Indian in English prose.

There is still, however, widespread opposition in India to remaining within the British Commonwealth. It was Nehru who insisted on retaining the link, from which he sees only advantages. The Prime Minister looks upon the Commonwealth as an international organization that works. Through its machinery, India has allies who can interpret her point of view to third parties. Encompassing members in Asia, Africa, and North America, the Commonwealth is a true bridge between East and West, transcending color lines and ignorant prejudices.

Nehru has found considerable value in the continuous interchange of views and information among Commonwealth countries, giving New Delhi what amounts to a world-wide intelligence service without cost. Finally, India belongs to the Commonwealth sterling bloc, with her currency backed by reserves in Britain. And, as proof that membership does not derogate from the freedom of action of any country in the group, there are the serious differences between India and fellow members—Pakistan, Ceylon, and the Union of South Africa. It is implicit in the arrangement that any country can withdraw at any time.

When it was decided that India should become a republic, in which the head of the state would no longer be a representative of the British sovereign, a tricky constitutional problem arose as to the Commonwealth tie.

India would be the only Commonwealth member not recognizing the sovereignty of the Crown. The problem was resolved by Nehru's agreeing that the Crown, while having nothing to do with the government of India itself, would be accepted as the symbol of Commonwealth union, with the monarch as titular head of the organization.

Since India became a republic on January 26, 1950, New Delhi has mourned the death of the late King and celebrated the birthdays of the young Queen faithfully and feelingly. The space given to the coronation in Indian newspapers was probably as great as in any of the Commonwealth countries that owe direct fealty to the Crown. There is reason to believe that in inventing the formula of a republic within the Commonwealth, India has shown the way to the two other Asian dominions of Pakistan and Ceylon.

The government of India was constituted on the federal pattern, with the twenty-nine states more or less autonomous. Education, law enforcement, public health, and numerous other spheres of government are the concern of each individual state, with the center administering the national interests such as federal taxes, customs, defense, communications, and so on.

There are serious flaws in this system, an example being lack of coordination between the state administrations and the Health Ministry in New Delhi in the attack on disease, a problem of greater importance in India than in perhaps any other country in the world. But in subjects like education and land reform, widely different situations and customs make it desirable to leave legislation in local hands.

Also because of varying conditions, the states of India are divided into three classes, A, B, and C. The A states are the former British autonomous provinces, comparable in political status with a state of the United States. The B states are autonomous but with a check on legislation by the States Ministry in New Delhi, while C states are administered directly from the federal capital through a chief commissioner. The latter two categories are made up of former princely territories and small units like Delhi, whose situation is something like that of the District of Columbia.

13

Journey to Nagaland

THE TALL, SUN-DARKENED MEN DRESSED ONLY IN LOINCLOTHS got off the train in Delhi station. A half-naked man ordinarily excites no notice in the streets of India's capital city. Occasionally one sees a *sadhu* (holy man) without a stitch on. Police discourage this these days, but the *sadus* are contemptuous of laws that run counter to their beliefs, one such belief being that clothing is an earthly link to be dispensed with, as a proof of being really out of this world.

The nearly naked men on the train aroused attention and curiosity, therefore, not because they were without any clothing but a scanty breechclout, but because they carried long, feather-tipped spears.

"Where is Jaipal Singh?" they demanded in Hindustani of the crowd at large. "We were told that all we had to do in Delhi was ask for Jaipal Singh, for everybody knows him." Then the gaping crowd understood that these were tribesmen from some remote part of India, because almost everybody did know that Jaipal Singh was the spokesman of India's plentiful but scattered aboriginals in Parliament.

No one looks or talks less like a tribesman than Jaipal Singh, an Oxford Blue, captain of India's world champion field hockey team in the 1932 Olympics at Los Angeles (India has never failed to win the championship in this sport at any Olympic Games), mainstay of the Delhi Flying Club, patron of sport, raconteur, and clubman. But the polished and handsome Jaipal Singh was indeed a tribesman from Ranchi in east central India, son of the turtle totem, picked up in the jungle by a missionary and sent on to a brilliant scholastic, athletic, political and social career, a favorite with Delhi hostesses as well as with his people in the forests.

"Where is Jaipal Singh?" the tribesmen from the train insisted, and someone went to a telephone. In a few minutes Jaipal Singh was at the station in his big American car.

Jaipal Singh's friends had never seen a train before they embarked on this journey to the capital. Totally unspoiled, their remarks on the customs and pretensions of modern civilization were pointed and pungent.

Shown Nehru's official mansion, they commented, "We thought these Congress fellows were supposed to be with the common people. Now we find they live like Rajahs." Taken to Parliament, they happened to arrive during a recess when many of the members were having tea and a snack in the Parliamentary restaurant. "These are the people who make the laws? All they do is eat," they snorted. Jaipal Singh had a hard time convincing them that the Hotel Imperial, where he was stopping at the time, was not his personal bungalow; they had never heard of a hotel. At the Delhi Flying Club they admired Jaipal's "estate," which happened to be the city's airport.

There may be thousands, perhaps millions, of tribesmen who think that Nehru, if they've heard of him at all, is some sort of Rajah. These are the earliest people of India, whose origins are largely unknown. Some came from Tibet, and in Assam there is an enclave of Mon-Khmers, descended from the vanished civilization that built the improbable magnificence of Angkor in far-off Cambodia. There are tree-dwellers, cave people, wild denizens of the hills and deserts, nomads, bandits, pygmies, head-hunters, tribes that hunt with the bow and arrow and spear, and some that know no kind of machine, not even the wheel.

There are several hundreds of tribes, in the wilderness all

over India. The tourist never sees them, unless he happens to be in New Delhi on January 26, Republic Day, for the annual tribal dance festival. But they number twenty-five million.

The Republic Day dance exhibition was instituted by Nehru, to help the people of India know each other. It is one of the rare spectacles that the country affords, with an astounding variety of primitive dancing, juggling and acrobatics. One year, at this show, many Indians learned for the first time that a true African tribe exists in Hyderabad. Descended from slaves imported by a Nizam of nearly two centuries ago, they have preserved their identity and culture intact through all those generations, an African enclave in India.

Usually not represented at these fiestas are the Criminal Tribes, whose ancestral occupations are robbery, swindling, and vice. These number about four million, mostly in the north, with half of them in Uttar Pradesh State. One theory of their origin is that they began as Rajput warriors defeated in battle and cut off from their social and economic moorings, to wander the countryside without homes or means of livelihood, and finally to turn to crime for a living.

The British concluded that these tribes were hereditary criminals with whom nothing could be done, so they labeled them Criminal Tribes and let the matter go at that. Every child born in such a tribe was considered destined to be beyond the law, and was treated as a confirmed miscreant from the time he could walk. Whenever practicable, such tribes were sequestered and kept under surveillance, with every male required to report regularly to the police, whether he had been convicted or even accused of an offense or not. His potential if not actual guilt was taken for granted.

An early reform under the government of free India was a program to rehabilitate the Criminal Tribes. First, the criminal label was removed, it being considered not only unfair but a distinctly self-defeating measure to brand an entire tribe with derelictions of ancestors. A government official in charge of the Criminal Tribes in Uttar Pradesh admitted to me that efforts to reclaim these people had suffered many disappointments, but he had hopes. Meanwhile, he added, the police continued to watch them carefully.

There are almost as many Criminal Tribes as there are crimes, for each has its specialty. There are numerous tribes of prostitutes, in which all the females engage in this profession. One tribe, whose women are famous for their beauty, works a variation: girls lure innocent villagers into a wood, where the bemused and unwary victim is set upon by men of the tribe and robbed, sometimes killed.

Another tribe, the evil Kabutri Nats, brings up its girls as marvelous dancers, almost superhuman in their acrobatic feats, and the boys as skillful pickpockets. While the dancers hold an entire village population spellbound, their little brothers slip through the crowd with light fingers, and their fathers and mothers loot the empty houses.

Some Criminal Tribes, near the big cities, specialize in swindling. A common and sure-fire method of mulcting unsophisticated women is to pretend to be a *sadhu,* work upon superstition to gain trust, and somehow acquire the household savings and jewelry. The most transparent schemes work regularly upon superstitious women, whose confidence can be won easily with a few simple feats of legerdemain claimed to be accomplished by divine power. The old ruse, far from unknown in the West, of "doubling your money" by putting it in a utensil and then leaving it for a few minutes while the "supernatural agent" works, is successful without fail in India in the hands of the clever swindler. Accounts of such cases, the trusting woman returning to find "*sadhu*" and money gone, appear in the papers with great frequency.

There are tribes of beggars, some practicing mutilation of children for sympathy; these can be seen a few steps outside the Hotel Imperial in New Delhi. Only a few miles from the capital is the village of snake charmers, where an entire tribe is brought up in this art.

The jungle tribes are one of Nehru's hobbies. He admires their dances and their unspoiled life, and takes a keen personal interest in their welfare. He is one of those who frown on bringing too much civilization too quickly to these people, forcing them to wear clothing, taking away the potent liquor that is part of their sustenance and important to their religious ceremonies. He prefers the simplicity of their life, he says, to the hurly-burly of the city with its stock exchanges and countinghouses, and he goes among them whenever he can.

In the wild northeastern hills of Assam the tribal territory is administered separately by the Northeast Frontier Agency, which, under the direction of the central government, is gradually bringing some measure of control into an area that the British marked off on their maps as "Unadministered Territory." The tribes, which here include authentic head-hunters, are permitted their own autonomous government under chiefs, with the smallest possible supervision by the agency under New Delhi.

This is highly strategic territory bordering Communist China, part of the vast area marked as Chinese on maps bearing the imprint of Peiping as late as 1954. Nehru has raised this territorial question several times with the Chinese Communist government, and the reply is always that these are merely copies of maps made during the Chiang Kai-shek regime. If that is so, one wonders why the Reds have not taken the slight trouble to change them since 1949. Nehru brushes off the question lightly when it is brought up in press conferences and elsewhere, and chided at least one Indian newspaperman for calling attention to the Chinese claim in a prominent and influential Calcutta newspaper.

Foreigners, and even Indians except on business in the national interest, are normally barred from all the northeast tribal territory, as they are also from crossing a line some distance back from the Tibetan border. But through

Nehru's personal kindness I was able to see a small bit of it in 1953, a rare privilege for a foreign newspaperman, and an American at that.

Of all newspapermen, Americans are probably the least welcome—excepting possibly Russians—in sensitive areas, for their writings are widely read, often reprinted in the Indian press, and they frequently write with an eye on political implications that Indians would rather not have aired. But aside from the restricted tribal and border areas, where even Indians are permitted only in exceptional circumstances, there is no attempt or even thought toward regulating the movements of any foreign correspondent anywhere in India. Nor is there censorship of any kind, or even scrutiny of a correspondent's dispatches before they go out, which is more than can be said of a number of nations counted as being in the free world.

However, when Adrienne Farrell of Reuter's and I showed up in Imphal, capital of Manipur State, to cover Nehru's conference with Prime Minister U Nu of Burma on common tribal border problems in April of 1953, it led to adventure with the tribes and a visit to restricted territory that we had not really expected to see.

Somehow Adrienne and I happened to be the only foreign correspondents interested enough in this story to make the trip with Nehru. Adrienne is a demure Irish-Belgian girl, only four feet ten inches tall in her flat-heeled shoes. A hand grenade is small, too, and if you were competing with Adrienne on a story she would probably be capable of breaking your arm. But I, being a one-newspaper "special" correspondent, was not competing with this wire-service fireball.

We were ahead of Nehru at Imphal. He sent his private plane from there to a strip on the Burma side of the border to fetch U Nu, and they held their first conference in the Indian town, ancient capital of the Maharajahs of Manipur and home of the famous Manipuri dances.

About 700,000 tribesmen inhabited the jungled hills of

the border area, approximately half on each side. There were a number of different tribes, but popularly they were referred to generally as Nagas. Naga means "naked," an accurate description in some cases. They moved freely back and fourth across the border, and occasionally there was an outburst of tribal warfare in which heads would be taken.

Nehru and U Nu had come to this remote country for a firsthand look at the situation, which was a joint problem, and also to talk over matters in general, as they did fairly often. The two Prime Ministers have a great affection and respect for each other. Nehru has consideration for his younger colleague, who is by no means a satellite to Nehru's neutralist philosophy, as many have believed erroneously.

Along with the Indian correspondents, Adrienne and I obtained permission to follow Nehru on his visit to the Nagas in the Kohima hill country. This preceded his meeting with U Nu at Imphal. The beautiful town of Kohima, high and cool, had been attacked by the Japanese in their farthest west penetration of India. The turning point in this theater of World War II came when the Japanese were defeated in the Battle of Imphal. Japanese skeletons are still found in the hills.

Kohima was the center of the "Nagaland" independence movement. While the countries all around them—India, Pakistan, Burma, and Ceylon—were being freed by the British, a number of educated Naga leaders headed by a man named A. Z. Phizo conceived the notion that the autonomous tribes, who had never really been ruled by anybody but themselves, also should form a sovereign state to be called Nagaland, and join the United Nations. Phizo and others had been to see Nehru, who dismissed them curtly and branded their idea as preposterous. Nevertheless, Phizo's organization, called the Naga National Council, maintained a more or less underground headquarters in Kohima and regularly turned out press releases detailing alleged instances of Indian police repression of the Nagaland movement, and bidding for foreign support of the tribal aspirations. Shortly after I last saw Phizo in New Delhi he disappeared, and was thought to be in hiding somewhere in Burma, where he also had tribal adherents.

Thanks to the work of Christian missionaries, many of them American Baptists, there was a considerable number of well-educated Nagas able to read, write, and speak English fluently. Some of them had been to the University of Calcutta. These young Naga intellectuals were in the forefront of the Free Nagaland movement. A group of them came to see Adrienne and me in Imphal to "extend the hospitality of Nagaland" to the foreign correspondents.

British officers and others, disgruntled with the end of their long reign in India, and foreign missionaries were blamed by the Indians for putting the idea of independence into the Nagas' minds. With the departure of the British, full suspicion fell on the missionaries, though bright young Communists from Calcutta, anxious to make trouble in any possible way, were also thought to be implicated.

Nehru himself was convinced that no Naga was capable of writing some of the petitions handed him over the signature of the Naga National Council, containing all sorts of citations from international law, scholarly historical references, and quotations from United Nations proceedings. The language of the documents led him to believe that some foreign agitators were responsible for their composition.

Having had perhaps more contact with the Naga agents myself than the official members of Nehru's entourage, I felt less inclined to dismiss out of hand the possibility that some of the young educated Nagas I met were quite capable of composing these letters unassisted, for they were a familiar type of youthful, burning intellectual, well schooled in political jargon.

At any rate, the American missionaries were under the deepest suspicion, and at least two of them were expelled from the tribal territory. This, I believe, was the genesis of the Indian government's present coldness to Western missionaries in general, which has caused some concern in Christian councils.

Nehru received his usual refulgent reception everywhere, and a big public meeting was arranged on the Kohima football grounds. While we were waiting for this to begin, Adrienne and I wandered among the several thousand assembled Nagas. We were immediately fastened upon by a group of the young Free Nagaland zealots and hustled before an assemblage of chiefs, resplendent in blankets somewhat remindful of the work of the southwestern Indians of the United States, wearing brilliant feather headdresses, and carrying shields and spears. The whole mob, which we estimated at about 3,500, was a most barbaric and picturesque spectacle.

Talking at length to the chiefs through our enthusiastic young interpreters, two things became plain. The first was that these proud tribal aristocrats felt no kinship with Hindu India at all. It was far easier, they said, to move from their native animism into Christianity than to try to adjust to the tortuous religion of the Hindus. And they thoroughly despised the acquisitive Bengalis, who as merchants and moneylenders were the hillmen's principal contact with the Indians of the distant plains. Secondly, there was a great deal more vigor in the Nagaland movement than Nehru seemed to think, whatever might be its merits. "Preposterous" or not, the dream was by no means confined, as Nehru believed, to a handful of crackpots around Phizo.

In a few moments Nehru was to have a dramatic demonstration of the strength of the Naga movement that must have shaken him no little.

While we were chatting with the chiefs, down on the football field, a delegation from the Naga National Council went to the speaker's stand with another petition for Nehru, and asked for an interview with the Prime Minister. Nehru would have seen them, he said later, but an officious deputy commissioner rudely put the delegation off. They returned grim and indignant, to the waiting crowd.

Before Adrienne and I were aware what was happening, the crowd began to melt away. "They have refused to listen to our case, so we are going," one of the young Naga interpreters told us. It was true; the entire assemblage of Nagas turned its collective backs on the speaker's stand and was slowly walking toward the other end of the field.

"Some of us are going to meet across the street," our interpreter said. "Come along and we will talk some more."

Adrienne and I thought this was a bad idea. Except for a few missionaries seated in the reserved section, we two were the only foreigners around. Foreign correspondents had already been accused, in the more militantly nationalist press as well as the strident Communist papers, of helping to foment the Naga dissidence. The last thing we wanted was to join in this walkout, conspicuous as we were with our white faces and khakis in that throng of brown, picturesquely attired tribesmen. There was no doubt that we would be accused by someone of encouraging the walkout for a story. As it turned out, we might as well have gone along, for we were named as the instigators anyway in several papers the following week.

It was a tremendous story without our help, though the Indian correspondents played it down. Nothing like this had ever happened to Nehru, since the time in 1946, before independence, when he was stoned by Moslem tribesmen in the Khyber Pass during the Pakistan agitation.

Nehru, accustomed to adulation everywhere, with hundreds of thousands spellbound by his mere presence, was looking at the Nagas' backs. As he began to speak, in English, the Nagas just kept walking away, following their chiefs silently, without a word or a shout, not even turning around to see what Nehru looked like.

No one stayed on the field to hear Nehru but a contingent of the Assam Rifles and perhaps three hundred Bengalis and the few foreigners in the reserved seats. There was not a real Naga to hear him except a couple who were interpreting and performing other duties at the speaker's stand.

Nehru was stolid under the blow, and delivered his speech. He dwelt at some length on the Naga agitation without referring to the walkout, and included a few pungent remarks about "foreign influences." That evening I asked him if he would elaborate on this, and I believe I got from him the first exposition of what was to be India's future policy on missionaries.

He began with a high tribute to the innumerable missionaries who had forsaken all the comforts of civilization to live in the wilds, dedicating their lives to the education and health of the jungle people whom everyone else had neglected. He was quite fervent on this subject, saying that India owed these missionaries a great debt, and that he wished their unselfish work to continue.

But religious proselytizing, he added, was a different matter. He had no objection whatever, he declared, to the spread of Christianity, which after all was an ancient religion in India. (According to tradition, the earliest Indian Christians were converted by St. Thomas the Apostle, in the first century A.D., long before Europe ever heard of Christianity, and centuries before Islam was invented.)

Medical and educational missions were all right, Nehru said, but the spiritual side must be left to Indian Christians, because it was not in India's national interest, in his opinion, for foreigners to exert a religious hold on nationals of the country. "They cannot possibly have an Indian point of view," he declared, "and it is not a good thing for a foreigner to exercise such an influence on the minds of Indians, instilling an outlook that is alien to us."

Shortly afterward, the government began refusing visas to missionaries who wished to come to India solely to make converts, but the others were allowed to stay.

In the months that followed, the Christian missionaries

were to experience some uneasy times. Aroused by publicity on the Naga incidents, the Hindu organizations launched a sustained campaign of accusations against missionaries, alleging economic and even physical coercion against villagers to join the church. There was a barrage of indignant questions in Parliament from the Hindu benches and the newspapers joined in with editorials, letters to the editor, and headlines.

Simultaneously the Arya Samaj, the one Hindu sect that goes in for proselytizing, opened a *Shuddhi* (reconversion) campaign to bring ex-Hindu Christians back into the fold.

The effect on the petty functionaries who handle immigration matters was unfortunate. Visas for missionaries returning from home leave or coming out as replacements suddenly encountered many complications. There was an outcry from the Christian organizations, whereupon the government was able to prove with figures that more missionaries had been admitted to India after 1947 than before. What it all appeared to boil down to was a new government policy that visas would be issued readily enough for replacements for the medical missionaries and teachers already in the country, but that henceforth evangelical work must be entrusted to Indian nationals.

India has about nine million Christians, of whom about half are Roman Catholics, with their own Cardinal as Archbishop of Bombay, a number of Indian bishops, and many Indian priests. In the south, along the Malabar Coast, there is a powerful Christian element of Jacobites, Syrian Christians, adherents to the See of Antioch, and others. There is a tomb of St. Thomas the Apostle near Madras, where his remains are said to be, and the Portuguese colony of Goa—once called the "Rome of the East"—enshrines the preserved corpse of St. Francis Xavier, which was formerly placed on view at intervals for Roman Catholic pilgrims from all over the world.

14

The Fight Against Caste

No doubt India has come some distance from the days when an Untouchable child was not permitted inside a schoolhouse with little Caste Hindus, but had to sit outside and listen to the teacher through a window. And when the Caste Hindu teacher wished to chastise an Untouchable pupil, he would stand at some distance and throw his cane or switch against the child, who would pick it up and toss it back after each blow. Thus was defilement avoided. Even after India became independent, I have visited a great university and found that the long refectory tables were cut into individual sections, with just enough space between that no one would be actually sitting at the same table with an Untouchable student, or one of lower caste.

The new Constitution abolished caste distinctions, and the Parliament only recently implemented this clause with a law prescribing penalties of fine or imprisonment for any practice of caste discrimination, but the institution of Hindu caste, so old that no one is sure how it originated, has not been legislated out of existence overnight.

All but the most orthodox Hindus agree that casteism is the curse of Indian civilization. There are some, like the late Gandhi, who contend that the original principle of caste was laudable, bringing a stratified order into Hindu society and allotting occupations. In time, they say, the system became corrupted and abused, surrounded by a welter of taboos and superstitious beliefs.

There is no doubt that caste distinctions are gradually dying out in the cities, but in the 550,000 villages, where 90 per cent of the population lives, the patterns of a thousand years ago are not essentially changed. Five miles outside India's capital city, I have visited a village where Untouchables and Caste Hindus draw their water from separate wells, and the depressed classes are confined to a noisome, objectionable quarter.

The castes are grouped into four broad divisions: the Brahmins, priests and teachers, who according to Hindu mythology sprang from the head of Brahma, the Creator; the Kshatriyas, princes and warriors, from Brahma's arms; the Vaisyas, merchants, from Brahma's thighs; and the Sudras, or menial workers, from the god's feet. Only the first three are of the "twice-born," entitled to wear the sacred thread, which the high-caste Hindu wears about one shoulder all his life. Ceremonial investiture in the thread is considered his second birth.

Each of these divisions has innumerable subdivisions. Ask a Hindu his caste, and he is likely to say Iyer, or Ayyangar, for example, instead of Brahmin. These are Brahmin subcastes. I never heard Gandhi described as a Vaisya, but always as a Bania. As one writer said, if there were a caste of chauffeurs, in time there would be subcastes of Cadillac drivers, Ford drivers, and so on. There are thousands of subcastes, each with a traditional monopoly on a certain type of occupation, with rules of conduct peculiar to itself, and preferring to marry within the group.

Below the four castes are the outcasts, or Untouchables. Some question has been raised as to whether they are even Hindus, since they were formerly barred from the temples (and still are in some places, contrary to law). But they certainly belong to the Hindu social order, and the Caste Hindus would find existence intolerable without the multitudinous services that only an Untouchable is permitted to perform. Among many odious types of work, the Untouchables alone handle refuse, work in leather, dispose of dead animals, and sweep the floors. Like the Caste Hindus, the Untouchable community is compartmented without limit.

Every household in India, regardless of the family's religion, has an Untouchable attached to it. He is the Sweeper, belonging to that subdivision of the Untouchables. As the name implies, he sweeps; and he also cleans the bathroom. He is an essential servant, and no one else will do his work, not even a non-Hindu, for converted Moslems and Christians take the caste consciousness of Hindu India with them to their new religion. My wife used to say that there were certain jobs around the place that only two people in the household would do: an Untouchable or herself.

Care of the bathroom, incidentally, follows a carefully prescribed pattern in those households, which are in the majority, that do not have modern plumbing. Every "dry bathroom" has two doors, one leading in from the rest of the house, another leading outside toward the servants' quarters. When you enter the bathroom, you close the outside door, preferably with a slam to alert the Sweeper. When you leave, you open the outside door and close the inside door after you. The next time you go in, the Sweeper will have been there. It is all as mechanical as pulling a chain and, in fact, more dependable.

Caste is a pyramid, with the Brahmins at the top. The Sudras, at the bottom, are by far the largest segment of the population. The Untouchables, who have no part in the pyramidal structure, number at least forty-five million, but there is a suspicion that the official estimates may have been weighted to make their total appear smaller than it actually is; there is some latitude in definition as to who is an Untouchable and who is not.

Economically, the Untouchables are frequently better off than the Sudras, for having an absolute monopoly on certain types of work that the community cannot do without. But socially the Untouchable suffers a disability unapproached by any other class of people on earth. To some orthodox Hindus the sight of an Untouchable within a certain distance away is a pollution.

The terrible thing about caste, to the non-Hindu way of thinking, is its inexorability. There is nothing a Hindu can do in this life to escape his caste, except to be outcasted for some violation of taboo, which is worse, for this puts him below the lowest of the low. Not only is he confined to his particular caste until death, but his children and his children's children to the end of time will be in the same caste. (There have been instances of caste changes—one cannot generalize about anything in India—but those were exceptional happenings.)

According to the Hindu philosophy, the body is a vessel for the soul. An Untouchable who has lived a worthy life may be reborn a Brahmin, but the child of that Untouchable's loins must also be an Untouchable, perhaps as host to a soul that had inhabited a sinful Brahmin in its previous life.

This endless cycle of reincarnation can only be broken when the soul has achieved such purity that it becomes one with the universe, part of the infinite being, relieved forever from the pangs of rebirth. The devout believe that Gandhi, already venerated as a saint in his lifetime, attained this state upon his death. Although Gandhi believed in caste, he was the champion of the Untouchables, whom he called *Harijans*, or Children of God. Dr. Bhimrao Ramji Ambedkar, the brilliant but bitter leader of the Untouchables, fell out with Gandhi on methods, but years later when Ambedkar, as Minister of Law, wrote the Constitution with its clauses barring casteism, it was Gandhi whom the outcasts could thank for having aroused the conscience of India to the appalling crime of Untouchability.

The yearly report of the Commissioner for Scheduled Castes and Tribes—"scheduled castes," pronounced "sheduled cawstes," is a time-honored Indian euphemism for Untouchables—is always a discouraging document to the opponents of casteism. The commissioner, L. M. Shrikant, calls it to the government's attention annually in this volume that conditions for the Untouchables in most of the country are little better than before. "They are worse!" says Dr. Ambedkar, without fail.

I believe that the Untouchables are neither so bad off as Dr. Ambedkar believes, nor so well off as some Congress leaders would persuade one. There has been progress.

The Untouchables themselves have been partly responsible for their failure to advance farther. Some resist change for fear that it will eventually mean losing their hold on the ancestral occupation. Others reveal a natural diffidence in asserting their new rights. Though they are permitted in the temples, they don't like to go there. They do not patronize Brahmin restaurants, as they are entitled to do, because they do not feel comfortable in the company to be found there.

And their economic condition and lack of education, coupled with the sense of social inferiority instilled into them for countless generations past, make it difficult for them to assert a new status in social levels heretofore beyond their reach.

The dyed-in-the-wool Brahmins in the villages have resisted the emergence of the Untouchables, not only because of orthodoxy, but also because certain advancements threaten their own ancient monopolies from which they derive profit. An example is the village well. The well of the Untouchables will be a poor one, invariably, while the Brahmin well will be the best. In time of drought, it is the Untouchable well that will go dry first. It is against the law to prevent the Untouchables from coming to the Brahmin well, but if they did, it would be polluted and the Brahmins would not use it. The solution found in some villages was for the Brahmin to dip his utensil into the well and pour the water into the Untouchable's vessel, thereby satisfying the law and not defiling the Brahmin well. But the Brahmin charges for this service, so much per dipperful, and the Untouchable is at his mercy. If he does not comply, the Caste Hindus are not averse to using physical force, and intimidation of police is also far from unknown.

In the Brahmin temples, restaurants, hotels, and other resorts in a city where the police are more likely to enforce the law, another way has been found by the Brahmins to perpetuate the caste barriers. A temple that Untouchables have entered is thereafter shunned by Brahmins, and automatically becomes an "Untouchables' Temple." And so on down the line.

During my seven years in India there were two outstanding instances involving the Brahmin sanctity of temples. One occurred in Mysore, when Mountbatten was still Governor-General. He and Lady Mountbatten paid a sight-seer's visit to the famous temple there, and days later it leaked out to the press that the Brahmins had washed the inside of the sacred edifice with milk and performed all the other elaborate rites of depollution. For even the great Lord Mountbatten was no better than any other creature without caste! Nehru, the Mountbattens' great friend, was furious and raised a tremendous row against the temple priests, but not even Nehru can move India's staunch, timeless orthodoxy.

The Mountbatten affair was regarded generally as amusing, but years later another temple incident shocked the slumberous conscience of all India and caused a brief national resurgence of sentiment on behalf of the Untouchables.

Acharya Vinoba Bhave, the famous ascetic and inventor of the land-gift movement, led a group of Untouchables to a great twelve-hundred-year-old temple in Bihar. His intention was a dramatic fracture of the caste taboo that had always held this temple inviolate. As Bhave and his crowd approached the entrance, they were set upon by the priests with sticks and stones, and the highly revered patriarch was brutally belabored and thrown off the premises like a common pariah.

This insult to Bhave awakened the urban intelligentsia to the fact that there still was an Untouchable problem. For a while there was a fury of activity on behalf of the depressed classes, but as usual, it died down.

No one knows how Untouchability began. It is most commonly thought that the institution started with the early Aryan invaders erecting these social bars against the dark-skinned population to preserve the purity of their own race. This theory is supported by the fact that Untouchables all over India are extraordinarily swarthy, almost black.

Dr. Ambedkar devoted a book to another supposition that they originated from what he calls the "broken men," remnants of defeated tribes who found themselves acceptable nowhere, and were forced to live on the outskirts of the villages, shunned and supporting themselves by scavenging, as is the case in many villages today.

But a new day is coming. The old Gandhian core of the Congress party, the Socialists, the Bhave movement, and the Gandhi groups are the propagandists for equality in hundreds of villages. In these organizations Caste Hindus perform the "defiling" tasks, eat in company with Harijans, and advocate intercaste marriage.

These are significant advances. When Dr. Ambedkar, political leader of the Untouchables, married a Brahmin girl, it was front-page news all over India.

"Interdining," as the Indian cliché goes, wherever it happens represents a remarkable breakdown in the old social stratification.

The average Westerner visiting India, especially if only for a short time, is not likely to become aware of the elaborate taboos on eating. The matter first came to my attention when I dined with a cosmopolitanized Indian diplomat one evening in Karachi. We both had steak, and I didn't realize the tremendous significance of this until he remarked,

"Not only would my mother be physically revolted at the mere idea of eating beef, but she would not even eat in the same room with you!"

Perhaps 60 per cent of Hindus eat meat. Brahmins are usually strict vegetarians, except the Kashmiri Pandits, the caste in which Nehru was born. There are varying degrees of vegetarianism, some shunning eggs while others will even eat fish. But no Hindu, except a small percentage of the very Westernized, will eat beef. I have determined that in many instances, where the person is not at all religiously inclined, there is a real physical distaste for beef, the result of an ingrained mental attitude like that of many Americans who cannot understand the French eating snails, the Chinese cockroaches.

The extremists among the vegetarians are the Jains, who claim that their religion is older than Hinduism. Jain priests will not ride in vehicles for fear insects may be crushed beneath the wheels, and as they walk, the pathway is gently swept in front of them to clear it of possible ants and other small life. They wear gauze across their mouths, so that no tiny living organism in the air may be inadvertently breathed in. The more Westernized Jains, who come largely from Rajputana and are notably successful in business, particularly the jewelry trade, find such precautions impracticable, but they observe vegetarianism strictly.

Westerners in India, generally speaking, have little intimate contact even today with the real orthodox group, mainly by the wish of the latter, who prefer to avoid non-Hindus as being ritually unclean. In profoundly orthodox Madras, I have occasionally observed a reluctance even on the part of some Brahmin newspaper editors of my acquaintance to shake hands. Before I learned to spare them this embarrassment, I caught one or two of them rubbing their palms surreptitiously on their garments afterward.

I found it more tactful not to offer my hand to a Hindu until he made the first move, and quickly became accustomed to beginning with the *namaskar*, the graceful Hindu gesture of greeting and farewell, made by bringing the hands flat together under the chin as if in prayer. Moslems raise the right hand to the forehead; political relations being as they are, it is best for the tourist to forget all about *namaskar* when in Pakistan!

Whether the Hindu religion, a remarkably flexible social system, will eventually dispense with caste is a question for future centuries to determine. Certainly it will not disappear entirely in one generation. But the struggle of India to catch up with the twentieth century in all fields is bringing a powerful influence to bear against the old ways in religion as in everything else.

For example, there is the increasing industrialization of India. There is no room for caste on the factory assembly line. And caste has no existence in the Army, where all live together.

Numerous fallacies supported by the British have been disproved in the post-independence reorganization of the Indian Army. One of these concerned the "martial" and "nonmartial" castes, the latter having been excluded by the British from the armed service as temperamentally unsuited to the military life. Free India opened the ranks to all, and it was quickly discovered that the "nonmartial" castes produced soldiers as good as any.

In the big cities, caste consciousness has been largely squeezed out of the shop, the office, the government bureaus, the educational institutions. In India, as elsewhere, the employment opportunities of the city are attracting more and more youth from the farms, who take modern ideas back to their villages. The blanketing of India by the village community projects program is also having its influence on the generation coming up, however stubbornly the oldsters may resist.

So the picture is both good and bad. Considering the nature of India, where a majority of the population is still not far removed from Biblical times, the progress made in a few short years has been, on the whole, remarkable. And the average Indian being an eager, adaptable person, modernization may be expected to be an accelerating process.

15

From Burqa to Ballot

MY WIFE AND I ONCE SPENT AN EVENING TEACHING A YOUNG Indian matron, who was going to the United States for the first time, how to shake hands with a man without seeming to be handing him a dead fish. Of the hundreds of Indian women we met, 99 per cent plus were shy and silent in the presence of men. Their marriages had been arranged by their parents in all but a very few cases, although the custom of choosing one's own mate is growing in the cities.

Universal adoption of coeducation, which presupposes a vastly wider spread of education itself in years to come, is probably the only development that will change the system of marriage.

"Westerners love and marry, Indians marry and love," said Dr. Pottabhi Sitaramayya, one of the doyens of the orthodox school in the Indian Parliament, when a bill was presented to liberalize the Hindu code of marriage and divorce. There is a lot of truth in it. An Indian girl is brought up to believe that she will love her husband, so she does, though she may have seen him only once or twice before the wedding ceremony, if at all.

American divorce statistics are cited triumphantly by the elders as proof that the Indian system is the best. Many progressive Indians are as skeptical as I am about this. Since divorce is not open to the orthodox Hindu wife, there are no significant statistics on broken marriages, but I know personally of so many bitterly unhappy Indian unions, and so many fine ones too, that I am inclined to think that prearranged marriages, on the average, promise neither greater nor less domestic felicity than our own free selection of mates.

"You Westerners take great care in breeding animals, but none whatever in the mating of humans," a well-traveled young Indian prince accused me once. I could see a point there, too. Careful selection, with the utmost attention to physique, mental qualification and family tradition, perhaps may be credited with having produced in India the most beautiful and intelligent of races.

Of course, there are homely Indians and stupid Indians, and such a one will probably draw a homely and stupid mate, unless wealth and position are involved, considerations which can outweigh any deficiency of mind or body.

The process of arranging marriages in India is highly standardized. When the boy or girl reaches marriageable age, the parents shop around, first among their friends. "Marriage brokers" are used extensively, too, and most Indian newspapers carry columns of matrimonial advertisements in the classified section: "Wanted: beautiful, fair-skinned accomplished Khatri virgin or issueless widow, age 18-24, for handsome Khatri bachelor, 28, matric, well-connected, government service."

A glossary may be needed for this ad. The lad wants a mate of his own Punjabi warrior caste; an "issueless widow" would probably be a child bride whose husband died before the marriage was consummated; and he is a "matric," which means he graduated from high school. In recent years fewer advertisements have specified caste, many stating "caste no consideration."

There is much negotiation before the marriage is agreed. Caste and family background being satisfactory to both sides, the astrologers must be consulted. If a casting of the two horoscopes indicates that the stars frown on this union, that ends the matter. The astrologer will also fix the "auspicious day" for the wedding, and no consideration will change it.

Once past the astrologers, the bargaining begins. The father of the bride offers a dowry, or it may be the other way around if the boy is ill-favored and aspiring to marry above himself. These negotiations may be long drawn out and most unflattering to the principals, whose every defect will be brought up in an effort to lower the dowry.

The dowry custom exerts such a pernicious influence on the economy of the country that two states, Punjab and Kashmir, have introduced legislation to abolish it, but the reform is meeting powerful opposition from moneylenders and also from fathers who have paid out large sums to marry off their daughters, and hope to get the money back through a son.

One wedding of a daughter may impoverish a family for two or three generations. The bride's father, besides paying the dowry itself, must outfit the bridegroom as well as the girl, and stand all expenses of the wedding, including the railroad fare of innumerable relatives and friends of both parties, and their keep for several days. Naturally every father feels compelled to put on the most extravagant feast he possibly can. Pending reform legislation on dowries also aims to limit the number of wedding guests and the amount of food they can be provided by the host.

The only unobjectionable feature of the whole procedure is that the possessions heaped upon the bride by her father, saris and ornaments, are supposed to be her nest egg for a rainy day.

I, as the father of three daughters, often thanked Providence that I wasn't born an Indian! My situation as a person of modest means would be utterly hopeless, with endless debt ahead, if I expected to make proper Indian marriages for Suzanne, Joan, and Stephanie!

Like many other needed reforms in Hindu society, the emancipation of women was stultified by the backwardness in which India was enslaved under colonial rule, until the period of progressive thinking among Indians themselves set in after the First World War. Since independence, with many women in Parliament, in provincial cabinets, and active in virtually every field of the national life, the emergence of women has doubled and redoubled its pace.

But, as in every other sphere, the problem in India is so vast that the gains made in the past few years, however great they may be, are likely to be lost to sight in the darkness of the picture as a whole.

The British, for political reasons, made it a point to leave Indian customs strictly alone, however objectionable they might be to the rulers. The one exception was the abolition of *sati,* the Hindu practice of widows immolating themselves in the flames of their husbands' biers.

That was in the eighties, yet even today isolated instances of *sati* occur, particularly in Rajasthan, and policemen who have tried to prevent the widow from throwing herself into the fire have been driven off by religion-crazed mobs, and even killed.

The self-immolation of widows, sometimes with assistance of solicitous in-laws if she faltered before the flames, is thought to have had an economic aspect, for in the orthodox family a widow is a burden to everyone, not least of all to herself. Forbidden to remarry, she is condemned to a life of hopelessness and scorn. The breaking down of this taboo is considered by many Indians as one of the most important steps forward in the whole program of equal rights for women.

Ever since independence, Prime Minister Nehru has been trying to force through Parliament the revolutionary Hindu Code Bill, a reform of all the laws relating to women. Clauses permitting women to sue for divorce on standard grounds such as are admitted in most of the world, and guaranteeing the right of widows and daughters to inherit property for the first time, have been passed against strong orthodox opposition. Women themselves were prominent in the agitation which has stalled the Hindu Code Bill and forced enactment of reforms piecemeal.

The chief arguments advanced against the Hindu Code Bill are that it will tend to loosen the sacred bonds of the sacrament of marriage, and break up the Hindu "joint family" system by providing that all shall share equally in inheritance. The traditional Hindu joint family is a unit to which all contribute and in which all share. The property belongs to the family as a whole, and is held by the head of the unit, usually the oldest male member. The relationship implies an obligation of the stronger to take care of the weaker, with the welfare of sisters being a particular charge upon brothers.

However well the joint family system may have worked over thousands of years gone by, and however desirable its continuance may be in the eyes of the orthodox population, it is plain that the end of the institution is at hand in the world of today. Statistics gathered by the Indian government have demonstrated that the old adherence to the joint family has been declining sharply for the past twenty years as new economic pressures, new opportunities, and a new outlook born of greater education have inclined more youths to leave the ancestral hearth and form their own households.

The famous institution of child marriage, for which there was also an economic reason, has been outlawed since 1929, but the 1951 census report estimated that approximately 9,200,000 Indian couples had been married between the ages of five and fourteen years, since the law was passed raising the legal age of marriage to eighteen for boys and fourteen for girls. Like other social evils of India that are hallowed by ancient custom, child marriage is not going to be abolished overnight simply by making it illegal.

I recall riding in an automobile with an alert young Indian nobleman, who suddenly called out, as we passed through a bazaar, "Stop the car! I want to buy some ice cream and balloons for my wife"—who was ten! The young noble was very fond of the youngster, and played with her as one would with a favorite child. Indian society does not countenance consummation of such marriages until the bride reaches an appropriate age.

Katherine Mayo's book, *Mother India*, the very mention of which is anathema in India to this day, is nevertheless quietly credited by many sober Indians with having speeded the abolition of child marriage. The 1951 census report states that although child marriage does take place in defiance of the law, there is "clear evidence" that the number is diminishing.

Polygamy, also on the verge of being outlawed, has been little practiced in recent years, not only for economic reasons but because gradually an odium has become attached to plural marriage. The monogamy law, when passed, may exempt Moslems, since their religion allows four wives.

I have not heard of any prospective legal curb on polyandry, the practice of taking plural husbands, which exists in the Toda tribe of the Nilgiri hills of south India, among some Sikh communities in the Punjab, and most prevalently with the hill dwellers along the borders of Tibet, where polyandry is the rule.

With the emergence of women in politics and other fields of public endeavor, one can see an end also to *purdah*, the seclusion of females behind the veil and the compound wall. Even in communities of strict Moslems, who introduced this custom to India, one sees fewer *burqa*, the cruel, tentlike garment that covers from head to foot, with a latticed slit for eyes.

Like the orthodox women who march in processions protesting the Hindu Code Bill that is designed to free them, some Hindu matrons cling to *purdah* as a "protection" rather than a stricture on their human liberty. I have known cases of women insisting on seclusion even against the wishes of their Westernized husbands.

But even women who cling to the *burqa*, either by choice

or family custom, formed up in the polling queues to cast their vote in India's first national elections. One successful candidate among many women was the shy, retiring Rajmata or Queen Mother of Tehri Garhwal, a Himalayan hill state, who had been in *purdah* all her life until she appeared on the campaign platform. Still one of the most orthodox of Hindu women, she is one of the most faithful attendants at Parliamentary sessions, and was one of three women Members of Parliament comprising an official good-will delegation to Japan. Within the Rajmata's lifetime, in the circles in which she moved, there was a time when crossing the sea, the forbidden "black water," would have meant excommunication from her caste.

Orthodox doctrines of Hinduism are explicit on the place of the wife in the background, and she is enjoined to worship her husband as a god. Yet the history of India contains many instances of women playing a decisive role in public life, as rulers and even as leaders of troops. Everyone in literate Indian circles knows the story of the heroic Rani of Jhansi, who commanded her soldiers against the British, and was killed in battle.

In older days, *purdah* was adopted as a protection. The Sikhs, I was told, only acquired the custom in recent times, when a wicked Maharajah of Patiala was in the habit of picking up any attractive girl he noticed and bundling her off to the palace. So the girls took the veil to escape the ruler's roving eye. The Indian girl of tomorrow will be more likely to rely on judo than the *burqa*.

16

The World's Most Democratic Election

The pattern of a new India was molded in 1951, when the first national elections were held, and the first Five-Year Plan was put into operation.

Everywhere except in Soviet Russia India's elections were praised as a remarkable demonstration of democracy. The Communists, who didn't make the showing they expected, complained that the balloting was controlled, and Tass, the Soviet news agency, accordingly cabled so to Moscow.

Actually, the Indian election was handled superbly under Commissioner Sukumar Sen, who later was borrowed to supervise the first voting in the Sudan. The system of numbering ballots, with the number of the ballot drawn entered opposite the voter's name on the roll, theoretically made it possible to tell how any individual voted. In practice, there was no allegation that the secrecy of the ballot box had been violated in any instance, as the boxes were locked and taken to another place to be counted in the presence of representatives of all the political parties.

With 83 per cent of the electorate unable to read or write, the ordinary ballot containing all the candidates' names could not be used. Instead, each party and independent candidate was allotted a box in the polling booth, with a symbol on it; Congress, for example, had two yoked bullocks, the Socialists a peasant's hut (which caused some confusion, because in various parts of the country the houses are different). The voter dropped his ballot in the box under the symbol of his choice. So that he couldn't possibly vote twice, his hand was daubed with a spot of special indelible ink guaranteed not to disappear in a day.

There were a number of invalid votes, however. For example, one honest old peasant who had promised his support to each of twelve candidates kept his word by tearing his ballot into a dozen pieces and dropping one into each candidate's box! And tens of thousands of women disfranchised themselves by refusing to give their names to the registration officer, in observance of a rule in some sects that a married woman's name can be spoken only to her husband.

The Indian elections were probably the most truly democratic ever held anywhere, for even the most primitive tribesmen were permitted to vote, and some of their number were elected to Parliament and state legislatures. It was as if an American election included the remotest Eskimo tribe of Arctic Alaska and the spear-carrying, grass-skirted natives of Yap Island. Even the head-hunters in the border hills could vote. Some entire tribes traveled for many days through mountains and jungles, pitching camp nightly on the way, to reach a polling place.

Eligible voters—all persons twenty-one years old or over, male or female, who were of sound mind—numbered 176,000,000. A statistician estimated if the electoral rolls, in a dozen or more languages, had been bound together they would have made a book twelve feet thick. Sixty per cent of this number went to the polls, a greater percentage than has voted in some elections in the United States.

The Indian election demonstrated that the people of the East, though they may be poor, illiterate, and barely clothed, are not lacking in political consciousness. Furthermore, the returns in India revealed a widespread understanding of what an election is for; in every state, how the parties lined up when the counting was over bore a distinct relationship to local conditions.

For example, in states like Uttar Pradesh, Bombay, and Mysore, where the incumbent Congress government had a good record of administration, Congress won hands down. In states where living standards were the lowest, the leftist parties made their best showing, as was to have been expected. And in former princely states, where Congress was notably inefficient and corrupt, the electorate showed where its preference lay by voting heavily for princes and other candidates put forward by the former rulers.

Covering the election in India was a four months' job. There were not enough qualified election officials to conduct the ballot simultaneously all over the vast country, and it would not have been desirable to have done so if it had been possible. Balloting in the sub-Himalayan hill districts had to be completed in October, before snow blocked the mountain trails. In the rest of the country, the mild winter was the best season, but the timing of crops, religious festivals, seasonal floods, and other factors had to be considered in making the schedule for each region.

There was a welter of political parties in the field, but in the next national election, to be held in 1956-1957, there will be only four contesting on a national basis, under the rule that to gain official recognition a party's candidates altogether must poll 3 per cent of the votes cast. The qualifiers were Congress, the Kisan Mazdoor Praja (Peasants, Workers, People's) party and the Socialists, who have since combined as the Praja-Socialists, the Communists and the Jan Sangh, a Hindu sectarian party.

None of these four parties can be counted as truly "rightwing." With the Communists as the furthest left, the others line up about as follows, reading from left to right: Praja-Socialists, Congress, Jan Sangh. The real rightists will be found among the independents, who together scored heavily in the polling. There are intermittent efforts to bring the nonaffiliated conservative elements in Parliament together, possibly in combination with the Jan Sangh, to form an organized conservative opposition to the socialistically inclined Congress regime.

A four-party pattern seems likely to exist in India for a long time to come. The Communists, Socialists, and Congress appear to be permanent fixtures, with no coalition likely, though the Congress and the Socialists might eventually work out a voting arrangement such as Nehru suggested to Jayaprakash Narayan. The Praja group in the present Praja-Socialist combination was formed by dissident Congress leaders who were dissatisfied with the slow progress of land reform and social legislation. With better organization, the Praja-Socialists may emerge as the Number Two party behind Congress, ousting the Communists from that position. The Jan Sangh, or whatever conservative party takes its place, will probably remain comparatively weak.

The Congress Party was formed in 1885 as a nationalist freedom movement. When it was transformed overnight into the ruling party of the world's second largest country, and the biggest of the democracies, adjustments in outlook were necessary. These are still going on. Since 1947 the party of Gandhi (who left it in 1934 but continued to guide policy) and Nehru has lost so much of its former hold that Gandhi once proposed that it be dissolved.

As the revolutionary standard-bearer, Congress rolls covered every shade of political opinion. After independence, those who did not agree entirely with policy or the way the party and government were conducted tended to break away, like the Socialist and Praja groups. It is possible that some adjustment in the Congress program would bring a number of the dissidents back. But the significant change was not loss of membership—at present the Congress has 16,000,000 members—but the forfeiture of the confidence of the masses. Complacency, incompetence, and corruption, in that order, quickly cost the Congress the place it once held in the hearts of the people.

But as Nehru has said in his campaign speeches, the Con-

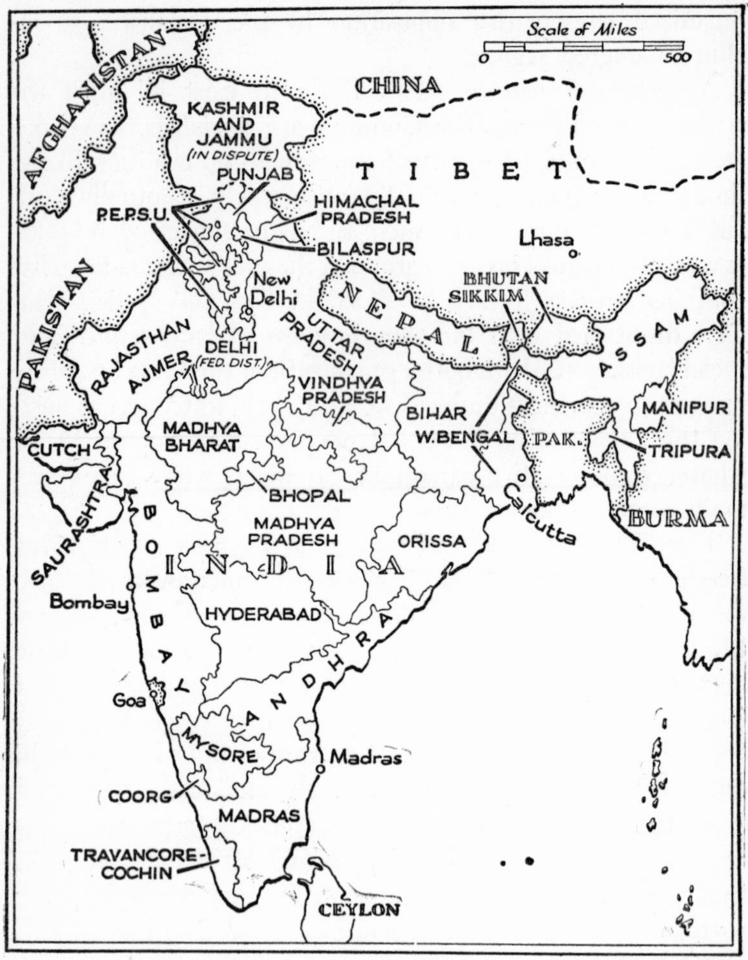

New York Times

PRESENT: The 29 states as they are today.

gress still has a far superior organization compared with that of any of the other parties, because it reaches into most if not all of the villages. In the 1951-1952 election, Congress won 362 out of 500 seats in the Lok Sabha (House of the People), the lower chamber in the Indian Parliament. (The upper house, the Council of States, is elected by the state

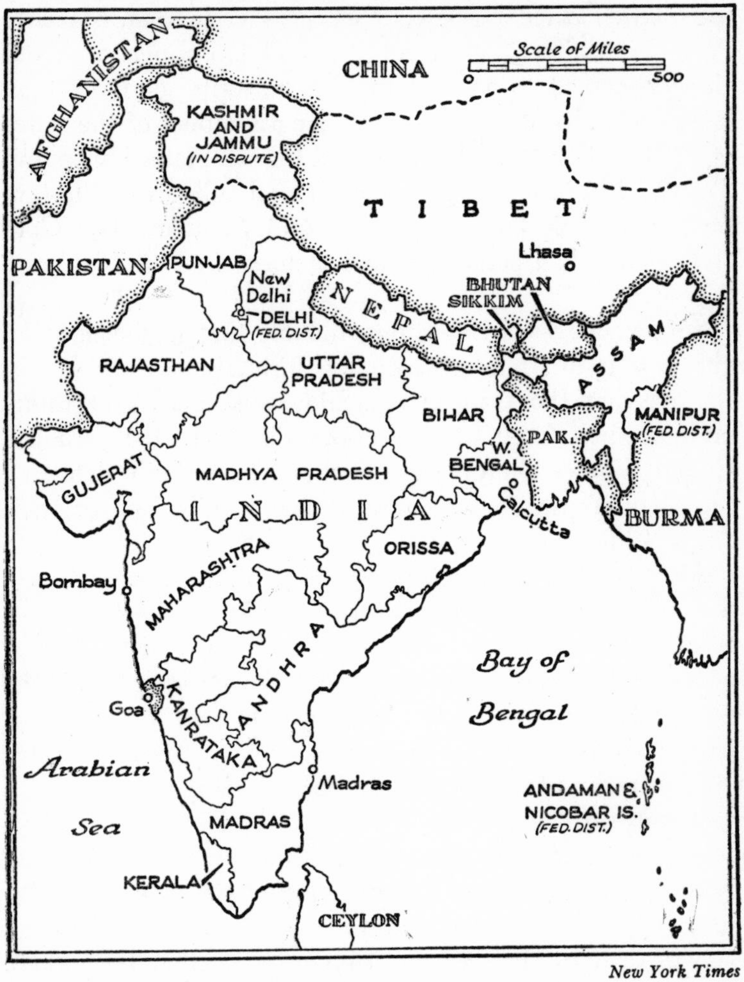

New York Times

PLANNED: The 16 states as they are projected.

legislatures except for a few seats allotted to the President for appointments to represent minorities and special groups, such as the arts. There are 100 members.)

Despite this overwhelming election victory, analysts professed to see a danger signal for Congress in the fact that the party drew only 44.9 per cent of the popular vote for House seats. Other percentages were Socialists 10.5, Kisan Mazdoor Praja party 5.8, Communists 5.4, and Jan Sangh 3.0. And Congress failed to win an absolute majority, or more than half the total seats, in the legislative assemblies of the states of Madras, Orissa, Patiala and East Punjab States Union and Travancore-Cochin, and in the electoral colleges of the centrally governed states of Tripura and Manipur. The Congress won only a perilously close majority in Hyderabad and Rajasthan.

Subsequent special elections, notably that in the new linguistic state of Andhra, which was formerly part of Madras, showed that the Congress machine was capable of canny politics when faced with a serious threat. In that instance Congress upset almost all predictions by soundly defeating the Communists in what was thought to be one of their strongholds.

After personally observing elections in many parts of India, my own opinion is that the continued dominance of the Congress party rests upon two factors: the establishment of efficient, honest government that can be seen by all the people, and the success of the Five-Year Plan in raising living standards.

The Indian voter, whether he be a peasant, a businessman, or a mill worker, supports the party that he thinks will give him good government and do everything possible to raise the generally miserable standard of living in the country, which many expert observers believe to be the lowest in the world. It was demonstrated in the 1951-1952 election that where conditions were relatively good, Congress won without difficulty.

As I toured Travancore-Cochin State during the campaign for the special election held there in February and March of 1954, it struck me that the Congress party would have had a much better chance if voting could have been postponed until all the development projects that I saw in action had begun to show results. Driving the length and breadth of the state, every few miles I would find roads being repaired, new roads being built. I stopped to look at an agricultural project that is expected to triple the yield of rice in one of the worst deficit areas. Everywhere in the state the government was doing something to better conditions.

But most of the projects were only in their beginning stages, and benefits had hardly reached the population, which is at the same time the most literate and one of the poorest in India. When the ballots were counted, the Congress had won only 57 seats out of 116 in the state assembly. Communists won 40, Socialists 19.

So this important southern state became the first in India with a leftist-labeled government. What happened was an odd political twist. The Communists and Socialists together were in a position to block the largest party, Congress, from forming an administration. So the Congress gave its support to a Socialist regime, in order to prevent the Communists from trying to form a cabinet. Eventually this peculiar combination fell, and Congress regained control.

The Socialists, in the 1951-1952 election, won nearly twice as many popular votes as the Communists, yet elected only nine candidates to the House, whereas the Communists brought in twenty-seven, plus at least eight fellow-traveling independents. It would appear, from these figures, that the Socialists scattered their shot. Another factor in the Socialist failure to make a stronger showing where it counted may lie in the fact that there is little ideological difference between the Socialists and the Congress.

The Congress program is itself strongly socialistic, advocating state control of basic industry and nationalization of numerous strategic enterprises. Nehru has stated his party's aim as being a socialist economy, but Nehru's terms must be defined by his own semantics. What he means here is not the complete nationalization of industry demanded by the standard Socialists, but a "mixed economy," to use one of his earlier phrases, in which private enterprise would have a place but would be controlled for the national benefit.

The process has already begun, first with enactment of a measure bringing all basic industries under government regulation, followed by the government's adoption of the steel expansion program, and most recently by the nationalization of a great banking institution.

Nehru's program doesn't leave the Socialists much except to argue that he should go even further. The Socialists also advocate severance of all connections with the British Commonwealth, and there the differences between the parties end.

But the Socialists, under the dedicated leadership of Narayan and brilliant, bearded Asoka Mehta, the general secretary, are strongly enhancing their following in the countryside, villages, and urban industrial areas through personal contact, taking up grievances, providing leadership for labor unions, and running model village and farm programs.

The Socialist party workers, young and old, carry on the unselfish service tradition established by Gandhi, whom they emulate in their way of life. They have gone in strongly for Vinoba Bhave's land-gift movement, of which more will be said, and the Sarvodaya or national uplift volunteer program. At the rate they are going they will soon have more direct contact with the masses than Congress does, if they do not already.

The witty and sharp young Socialists like Asoka Mehta have a gift for putting the party in the forefront of causes likely to gain helpful publicity. An instance, in 1954, was the Socialist sponsorship of the case of poor, landless peasants in the grasslands of Bombay State. In a certain area a great deal of acreage is devoted to raising grasses for pasturage, which the villagers customarily reap every year for a payment from the owners of the land. Anyone who has been around India will surmise that this payment is absurdly small.

When the time came to cut the grass in 1954, the peasants, egged on by the Socialists, refused to work. Furthermore, they swarmed onto the fields in hundreds, with Socialists foremost, and began breaking the ground with plows and spades for sowing crops to relieve their food shortage. Landlords called the police, who ordered the embattled peasants to throw down their implements. No one paid attention, so the police went into action. But no sooner did a policeman force a peasant to drop his instrument than another peasant would pick it up and start working behind the policeman's back. It ended with the arrest of scores of Socialists, including Mehta. After a brief time in relatively luxurious and polite imprisonment, they were released.

This sort of thing delights the ordinary Indian, who hates landlords and police on general principles. And such a movement was exactly the kind of technique Gandhi employed against the British, with his civil disobedience campaigns and his famous march to the sea to make illegal salt.

The Socialists, and in fact many others, such as disgruntled student groups, frequently seize upon the Gandhian method to embarrass authority. As Gandhi must have calculated, there's something in non-violent defiance of law that appeals to the Indian nature. And it is extremely difficult for the law to cope with it. Police have sometimes thought to discourage such demonstrations by loading the offenders into trucks and releasing them miles from their homes, leaving them to walk back under the frightful Indian sun.

But Indians do not mind suffering. In fact, I think they like it.

17

Crazy, Mixed-Up Communists

When I try to think of one phrase to describe India's Communist party, a bit of current American juvenile slang comes to mind. They are "crazy, mixed-up kids," hopelessly divided among themselves and pursuing the line of action least likely to succeed.

Communism is an alien philosophy entirely at variance with Indian patterns of thought and action, and the Indian Communist movement does not include a single individual whose name fires the imagination. The party has piled up an unparalleled record of ineptitude and failure since it was founded in 1925, and its current status becomes insignificant when compared with Communist strength in such countries as France and Italy.

Of course, no Communist conspiracy anywhere can be entirely discounted, and the Nehru government is far from complacent about the party's activities in India. At one time there were more than 10,000 Indian Communists in jail, and all Reds are closely watched today. The party claims a membership of 60,000, a decline of 25 per cent since the last previous announcement, which is minuscule in a country of India's population.

There can be no accurate estimate of the number of fellow travelers, but in any case I believe that the publicity given to the Indian Communist activities, both at home and abroad, leaves a grossly exaggerated impression of their influence on the country as a whole.

My own estimate of the Indian Communist strength, as I was preparing to leave the country, was that it is gaining among the youthful, the ignorant, and the woolly intellectual elements, but losing heavily among the influential strata of society. One evidence of this is the noticeable change in the attitude of many important newspapers, which are devoting an increasing amount of space to anti-Communist editorials and letters, which are particularly significant.

The Communists' most effective enemy has been Jawaharlal Nehru. In desperation, the Reds have come around to endorsing most of his policies. This tactic, however, will probably have little effect but to expose their weakness.

Nehru, in his election campaigning through the southern states where the Communists are strongest, put his finger on the party's one weakness that is most calculated to alienate the sympathies of Indians. This is the subservience of the party to a foreign power, namely the Soviet Union. India has been too recently freed from one colonialism not to be extremely sensitive to any possibility of another.

Noticing the Communist hammer-and-sickle flags flying from palm trees along his route through Travancore-Cochin, Nehru pointed to them, laughed heartily, and demanded of his peasant listeners, "What is that foreign flag doing over Indian soil?"

That hurt.

There was a similar reaction by the public at large when Communist Members of Parliament obtained allotment of a group of houses around Windsor Place, the most prominent intersection in New Delhi's best residential neighborhood, ran up the red flag on a high standard, and had stationery printed giving their address as "Red Square." Communist bluster, in answer to public questions, that the red hammer-and-sickle flag was the "international banner of the working classes" evoked only ridicule.

The average Indian being an extraordinarily skeptical individual, with a taste for biting humor, it could be that ridicule will be the weapon that will keep the Communist party of India from ever gaining nationwide respect.

It was particularly tactless and inviting of scorn, it seemed to this observer, when the Cominform sent Harry Pollitt, an Englishman, of all people, to dictate policy to the Indian Communist party's Third Congress in Madura, Madras State, in late 1953.

The continual stream of Indian Communists and well-known fellow travelers from New Delhi to Moscow and back serves to keep alive the widely held conception that the party is governed from the Kremlin.

The term "national" is one of the key clichés in Indian political thought. Nehru has spoken thousands upon thousands of words, in all parts of the country, to prove that the Indian Communist party, indeed all Communists everywhere, is "anti-national." The record bears him out.

The Communists, both in India and in Moscow, have misread Indian thought to an amazing degree from the beginning. In 1928, three years after the founding of the Indian Communist party, the Sixth Congress of the Comintern ordered its agents in India to drop the nationalist struggle against Britain, and concentrate instead on class war aimed at the "bourgeoisie." It happened to be the "bourgeoisie" that led the Indian National Congress at the spearhead of the freedom movement, and attacking this class was the most unpopular move that could have been chosen. But the Indian Communists dutifully and futilely followed the party line for six years, during which time they made the further gross tactical error of opposing Gandhi's civil disobedience movement begun in 1930.

When the error penetrated Moscow's consciousness, finally, in 1934, the party did a characteristic about-face and threw its support to the Indian National Congress, with the intention of infiltrating. That promptly brought down the wrath of the British, who banned the party.

The tortuous convolutions of Communist policy in World War II did permanent, irreparable damage to the party's prestige in India. When the war broke out in 1939, the Communists opposed Indian support of Britain's cause on the grounds that this was an "imperialist war." The Congress also opposed the war, but for a different reason, declaring that India would participate with the British only as an independent country.

Then when Hitler's Germany suddenly attacked Russia, the "imperialist war" was transformed overnight into the "people's war," and the Communists rallied to Britain's support. To the everlasting misfortune of the Communists, the British lifted the ban on their activities in India at about the same time that Gandhi, Nehru, and the core of the Indian nationalist movement was jailed for the duration.

Patriotic Indians have never forgotten that the Communists betrayed the nationalist cause on orders from Moscow.

Another tactical error of major importance emerged from the famous Communist policy meeting held in Calcutta in February 1948, under the guise of a "Southeast Asia Youth Conference."

It was at the Calcutta conference that the policy of violent uprising was decided for India and Southeast Asia. In addition to standard tactics of strikes and sabotage, the Indian Communists decided to borrow the method used successfully in China to turn agrarian unrest into an armed revolution. As their Yenan they chose the oppressed, poverty-ridden Telengana area of Hyderabad State, then still under the Nizam's rule. This seemed to be perfect ground. Perhaps it could have been but for another superb miscalculation of the Indian state of mind.

There are still many wild parts of India where policing is thin, where it is possible to set up a parallel government in defiance of the state's writ. Natural obstacles and the remoteness of the country, coupled with poor communications facilities or none, hamper and delay the inevitable retribution of the Indian government's soldiers and police. Such an area was Telengana, a name given to the Telegu-speaking portion of the Nizam's dominions.

The Communists made Telengana a little soviet, taking over hundreds of villages and redistributing the land among the peasants. This might seem to be a program calculated to win immense popularity, but instead it emphasized the features of Communist rule that were certain to alienate the countryside.

During the months that the Reds were supreme in Telengana, the area came under a reign of terror worse than the oppressed villagers had ever known before. Persons suspected of informing against the Communists were summarily executed, houses were burned, and even harmless grandfathers and grandmothers were ruthlessly killed when the Reds decided to penalize a village.

Such violent methods revolted the country's masses, who had been trained in the Gandhian philosophy that the means employed to reach an objective must be as moral as the ends. The conflict between communism and Gandhism was by no means an unimportant factor in alienating the peasant population against the Reds. In due time Telengana was brought under control, and the brief Communist rule is remembered as a time of horror.

Again seeing their error, the Communists now renounced violence as a policy, and asserted that they would seek to attain their aims by constitutional means through the polling booths. The election was then approaching.

Nehru, possibly with more prescience than idealism, ordered that the ban put upon the party in a number of states be lifted, so that the Communists could openly contest the elections. Through his intercession the party was made legal again everywhere in India except in the former princely state of Indore.

But not all imprisoned Communists were set free. The Preventive Detention Act, under which an individual could be taken into custody merely on suspicion that he might be contemplating an act against the security of the state, had been strengthened. Under the British, such a suspect could be held without trial for six months; free India made it twelve months, with the proviso that grounds for detention must be justified before a judge.

The Reds fought the elections unscrupulously. For example, in Hyderabad Communist electioneers would descend upon a village, make a list of the landless peasants, then draw up a schedule of allotments of lands and houses to be made if the Communists won. Many were gullible enough to believe such promises, and there were instances of Communists being elected while still behind bars.

When all the returns were in, out of 3,782 seats at stake in the elections to the national Parliament and the state assemblies, the Communists and allied fellow-traveling parties won around 250, while Congress took 2,600, or ten times as many.

Nehru's confidence that he could handle the Communists in an appeal to the electorate was further justified after the handful elected took office. Contrary to expectations, they showed up poorly in parliamentary debate, which in India is of a high order. The Communists' slavish adherence to the Moscow line, and constant belaboring of the "Anglo-American Bloc" with the usual clichés of the "fascist-imperialist-warmonger" type, became irrelevant and ridiculous.

The Communists had a real chance to demonstrate what they could do to improve conditions on at least a local scale when they won control of a number of municipalities in Travancore-Cochin State. Again they failed, through inexperience and confusion, and in subsequent municipal elections the Red administrations were mostly thrown out in favor of a return to conservative methods.

Meanwhile numerous schisms developed within the party. The old moderate wing, headed by P. C. Joshi, was ousted in the adoption of the ill-advised policy of violence in 1948, but was still on the side-lines. The extremists led by B. T. Ranadive had been discredited by the failure of the Telengana experiment. Among those that were left, a strong element with Rajeshwar Rao, an Andhra leader, as spokesman, dared to disagree with the party line that the United States was the first enemy. The Rao group contended that so far as India was concerned, the foe was "British imperialism" exercised through commercial investment.

At the Madura convention, with Harry Pollitt arbitrating, a compromise line was reached under Ajoy Ghosh as secretary-general. But the ultimate result of this attempt to repair the party front was another fiasco in public relations. For it soon came to light, through the efforts of busy anti-Communist elements centered in Bombay and elsewhere, that behind the official public pronouncement that the party intended henceforth to pursue its ends peacefully by the same constitutional means open to all, there was a secret manifesto setting forth violent revolution as the eventual means by which the Reds planned to take over India. The legal activities were mere camouflage for the real program of armed rebellion.

The success of Nehru's neutralist policy in the cold war proved another embarrassment to the Communists, who had been attacking the Prime Minister since 1948 as a "running dog of the imperialists." At about the time that these assaults on Nehru's foreign policy began to appear absurd even to the Communists, the national development program built around American-aided community projects began to take hold of the public imagination, and it became unprofitable for the Reds to continue their economic line of attack, too.

The Ajoy Ghosh leadership took the most sensible alternative, humiliating as it was, of endorsing Nehru's foreign policy and even the community projects, with a few vague and inconclusive reservations meant to be face-saving. After the exchange of visits between Nehru and Chou En-lai, the Premier and Foreign Minister of Communist China, and Nehru's triumphal journey to Moscow where his neutralist foreign policy was enthusiastically endorsed by the tutelary deities of world communism, the Indian Communist party sheepishly came out with a solid declaration behind its arch-enemy.

Indian communism's woes have been many at the hands of Nehru's government. An important source of revenue was removed when sale of its propaganda literature was barred from the book and magazine stalls of the railroad stations. The centralization of parliamentary activities in New Delhi around "Red Square," née Windsor Place, was broken up by inflexible application of the priority rule in allotment of housing to Members of Parliament. There is reason to doubt that anything goes on within the party that the Home Ministry, which is in charge of security, does not know.

The alleged joys of life behind the Iron Curtain began to be doubted seriously when two ambassadors from Czechoslovakia in succession quit their embassies in New Delhi and sought sanctuary in the West, one in Canada and his successor in England. It just happened that these two gentlemen were the most popular and widely known diplomats in India in their time.

But it must not be assumed from all the foregoing that the Communist party of India is without vigor or following, despite its reverses. With the schools and universities turning out hundreds of thousands of educated youths every year who cannot find suitable jobs, youths often well read in Marxism and frequently already indoctrinated in communism by the university radicals, the Communists are supplied with a bottomless pool of potential recruits. The "pink" intellectuals, artists, and writers, the India-China Friendship Association and various other "front" groups serve the Communist interests well, if sometimes innocently.

All Communists are cleverly schooled in propaganda, and the Indians are no exception. The numerous organizations for "peace" and banning the atomic and hydrogen bombs have potent voices in India, and all are Red-tinged. In labor organizations, though the Communists are not without strength they are far outdistanced by the unions dominated by the Congress and Socialists. In the field of cultural approaches and the exploitation of Asian suspicion of the white race, especially of Americans, the Communists have been outstandingly successful. Cultural bonds with the Communist nations have been forged artificially by means of exchanges of exhibitions and performers.

The Indian Communists, financed by the cheap sale of expensive Marxist literature supplied free through the Russian Embassy diplomatic pouches, have struck telling blows in the countryside through traveling groups of players who bring entertainment into the drab lives of the villagers. In their comic plays, which by village standards are really expert and extremely funny, the villain and the butt of the joke is always an American. The ordinary villager's love of popular music, Indian style—he is always humming the latest hit tune from the Bombay movie studios as he tills his field—has been seized upon to circulate light, catchy ditties with an anti-American, pro-Communist slant.

The United States Information Agency cannot compete on the village stage or in the composition of Indian tunes to get the villagers singing for democracy. The U.S. Information Service libraries are powerful influences, and the technical and informational films and slides distributed wholesale by the U.S.I.S. no doubt also gain an enormous amount of quiet publicity for the American way of life and what it has to offer India.

An unlimited expansion of the cheap book program to

match the Communist output of beautifully turned-out volumes at ridiculous prices would be a valuable outlet for the American message; books on technical subjects, and serious literature, are in tremendous demand, but regular publishers' editions are out of reach of the average Indian pocketbook.

A study of communism at work in India presents a mixed picture, and not one to be viewed with complacency. But there is no justification for some of the hysteria that appears in some of the appraisals of Indian communism reaching the United States.

Any American traveler in India who concentrated on the universities, the fellow-traveling groups, and the parlor-pink politicians and intellectuals might well be so dismayed as to leap to the conclusion that India is about to "go Communist" any day now. If he listened to the statements of Nehru on the "cold war" and related matters, without making a profound effort to understand the background of what Nehru says and what he really means, such an observer might believe that Indian foreign policy follows the Communist party line far too closely for American comfort.

But before making up his mind that India is all but lost to the Reds, the American observer should ask these questions:

Who are the Communist leaders in India? Is there even one, like Nehru in the Congress party, Narayan in the Socialists, and dozens of others that could be listed, whose name is in any way associated with the past aspirations of the Indian nation?

What sort of people form the rank and file of the Indian Communists? Are they the calm, sober element likely to gain respect in India's 550,000 conservative rural villages? What motivated them to join the Communist party? With alternatives at hand, are those motivations sufficient to bring millions of other Indians behind the Communist program, and if so, why haven't they done so?

What does the average Indian want his country to be? Is

he more likely to look to the new and foreign doctrine of communism than to Nehru's kind of democracy for the satisfaction of his wants? Does the age-old Indian social pattern, with its attachment to the land and family and the acquisition of personal wealth, readily adapt itself to a communistic outlook?

On a sober analysis of trends in Indian public opinion, does it appear that the Communists have gained or lost in influence in the last five years?

I do not believe that the answers to these questions are discouraging.

18

And on the Right We Have—

AT THE OPPOSITE END OF THE INDIAN POLITICAL SCALE FROM the Communists, the so-called Hindu "rightist" parties exercise an influence that cannot be ignored, because they represent the traditionalists, the protagonists of Sanskritized culture and a return to the values in Hindu ethics that have endured for thousands of years. They appeal unscrupulously to religious clannishness for political purposes.

These groups produced the fanatics that slew Gandhi. They also include some of the sharpest brains in India. Their outstanding leader, the late Dr. Shyama Prasad Mookerjee, was easily the most effective orator in the Indian Parliament, far better at marshaling his arguments and expressing them than Nehru, whose unedited speeches, almost always made extemporaneously, tend to be disorganized and repetitious. Dr. Mookerjee, a prominent educator in Bengal before he entered public life, was a great scholar whom Nehru held in high respect although he sometimes seemed to regard the ideas that Mookerjee represented as more dangerous than communism.

The Hindu parties are important for several reasons. One is that they are the political organs of certain substantial business interests that are not without power in their communities. For another, they take the lead in anti-Moslem and anti-Pakistan movements, always a potentially explosive influence. Finally, they are strongly anti-Communist.

Nehru devoted almost his entire personal campaign, in the 1951-1952 election, to fighting these parties, even in parts of the country where their influence did not extend significantly. This was at a time when grievances against Moslem Pakistan were much in mind, and not many months after some circles had talked of war to avenge the wrongs suffered by Hindus in East Pakistan. The crusade led by Nehru sent the Hindu parties down to a crushing defeat, only one, Dr. Mookerjee's Jan Sangh, winning the necessary 3 per cent of the votes to qualify as a national party.

If the several Hindu parties, and the many successful independent candidates of like mind, had been banded together under one party label, they would have shown a higher percentage of the popular vote than was won by the Communists. And despite their weak showing in the national election, they were able to raise such powerful public demonstrations, such as the one in Jammu against Sheikh Abdullah, that the government found it necessary several times to jail many of their leaders under the Preventive Detention Act. Dr. Mookerjee himself was in preventive detention in Kashmir when he embarrassingly died in 1953. His death while in government custody raised a national furore that lasted for months, in an effort to make him a martyr.

The economic program of the Hindu parties is not greatly to the right of the Congress platform. The chief characteristic of these groups' policy is a demand for a firmer line toward Pakistan, and recognition of the essential Hindu character of the Indian nation. While they make a pretense of encouraging Moslems to join their organizations, what they really stand for is a Hindu state, not necessarily theocratic as such, but following a policy of "Hindus first."

The Rashtrya Swayamsevak Sangh or R.S.S., already mentioned as prominent in the pogrom against Moslems in 1947, is the militant arm of the Hindu "rightists." They are headed by an anachronistic figure, the bearded *Guru* M. S. Golwalkar. Though Nehru and others of liberal strain dismiss Golwalkar as a fanatical clown, it is nevertheless a fact that his arrivals and departures at the Delhi railway station bring out huge crowds of followers.

In assessing the importance of this it must be taken into account that the refugee-swollen population of Old Delhi is a hotbed of bitterness against Moslems, at whose hands the refugees suffered in Pakistan, and against the Nehru government for not satisfying the refugees' more extreme demands. Golwalkar's stronghold is in the central Indian area extending north and eastward from Bombay, where many Hindus appear still to be living in the days of the great Mahratta leader, Shivaji, and nurture his militant spirit.

After the assassination of Gandhi by the fanatic Nathuram Vinayak Godse, who came from the Shivaji country and belonged to Dr. Mookerjee's original organization, the Hindu Mahasabha (Great Society), the Mahasabha and the R.S.S. were outlawed by the government. As always happens with Indians when their wrongdoing goes too far, there was a deep resurgence of public conscience, and for a time the two related societies were extremely unpopular. But, as usual again, the hysteria did not last more than a few months, and they re-emerged.

In an eventual breakup of the Congress machine, it is not inconceivable that the ultraconservative element in that party would find attractions in joining with the Mahasabha, the Jan Sangh, or whatever Hindu organization may have developed by that time.

Although these groups do not have significant political strength at this time, it should not be forgotten that their roots are in the mainstream of orthodox Hindu thought, and that they thrive on the easily aroused emotions of a deeply religious and volatile people.

The really conservative element in India, apart from the big business and banking circles, lies in the armed services. In comparative estimates of the armed strength of different nations, India always seems to be overlooked. Yet India has a thoroughly well-trained, highly disciplined, well-equipped, and unquestionably loyal army of about half a million, and is building a reserve corps of about a million more.

Man for man, the Indians may be the most powerful army in free Asia, with a constantly expanding air force above them, and a hope that the natural growth of the Indian shipbuilding industry will provide at least the necessary logistic support on the seas, if not a combat navy of significant strength.

The possibility is perhaps very remote, but there are some observers, both Indian and foreign, who believe that if prevailing political influences in India became so unwholesome as to threaten complete destruction of the country's welfare, an army coup is not out of the question.

19

Recollections of Gandhi

"SAURASHTRA," SAID THE PORTLY JAM SAHEB OF NAWANAGAR, "is famous for two things, lions and the Jam—that's me."

My quest for Bhupat, Saurashtra's desert Robin Hood who was charged with eighty-eight murders, led me to the Jam Saheb but not to the vanishing lions of the Gir forest. The fabulously wealthy ruler, whose odd title was derived from Iran, was then president of the United Nations Tribunal in New York, as well as Rajpramukh of Saurashtra State, a union of 489 princely territories.

Nothing came of the Bhupat investigation but a fine friendship with a remarkable young police officer named Aswini Kumar, the present-day Punjabi counterpart of the shooting U.S. marshals of the pioneer West. Aswini's specialty was running down *dacoits* (bandits) like Bhupat.

A first-class *dacoit*, Aswini said, never surrenders. When surrounded, he will invariably shoot it out, and either escape or be taken dead. Aswini, then only thirty-two years old, had already killed eighteen such desperadoes in gunfights. He had been transferred temporarily to Rajkot, capital of Saurashtra, from Simla to direct the operations against Bhupat's gang of cutthroats.

His investigations turned up a romantic conspiracy among some dispossessed princes of the area to regain power through the *dacoits*, who were terrorizing the countryside with the princes' assistance. They were just a few years too late.

The Rajkot jail soon acquired some colorful royal lodgers, but not Bhupat. India's most notorious bandit chief eventually escaped across the border to Pakistan, where he was sentenced to a year's imprisonment for violating the immigration rules and for carrying concealed weapons!

I heard of another *dacoit* in the Rajasthan desert who owned the world's only carnivorous camel. Forage being scarce in the sandy wastes, the animal learned to subsist on goat's flesh.

It was just another of the routine incongruities of a correspondent's life in India that I should have fallen into reflections upon Mahatma Gandhi while composing a story about a murderous desert bandit, with my battered Hermes typewriter resting on a desk of solid silver. My headquarters for the Bhupat interlude were in the former palace of the Nawab of Junagadh, converted into a Saurashtra State guest house. There was no place else to stay in Rajkot.

I got to thinking about Gandhi because Rajkot was not far from his birthplace, Porbandar, where his father had been *dewan* to the local ruler. This part of western India, called Gujerat, was full of associations with the great leader, and some day, perhaps, will be a place of pilgrimage.

It had been my good fortune to meet Gandhi briefly on three occasions in New Delhi, twice in the Bhangi Colony and once at the home of the capitalist, G. D. Birla, where he was killed. I remember the last conversation best, because in it Gandhi revealed a side of his character that has been little publicized. This was his sense of humor.

On Gandhi's seventy-eighth birthday, October 2, 1947, his last birthday on earth, I went around to Birla House to try to ascertain the state of the Indian patriarch's mind on passing another milestone. He was out somewhere, and I waited for his return. As he stepped from his car I pushed to his side and asked if he would make a birthday statement.

"Birthday?" he said, assuming an expression of puzzlement. "Whose birthday?"

"Why, uh, yours, sir," I stammered. Gandhi chuckled, his eyes twinkling mischievously over his drooping spectacles.

"Who told you this is my birthday?" he demanded. "Every day is my birthday! And yours, too. Every day, you see, we are all born again, we start a new life every day."

His ubiquitous young grandnieces, one supporting him by each arm, began to move impatiently and Gandhi drifted away, smiling with delight at his gentle joke.

Later I was told how, many years before when he was in London, Gandhi had asked to meet Charlie Chaplin. As the story goes, Gandhi kept the great comedian doubled in laughter for an hour with joke after joke.

Indians were very sensitive where Gandhi was concerned. It was about this time that I was called on the carpet by the Secretary of Information—the only time such a thing ever happened to me in India—for mentioning casually in a story that Gandhi was living in the mansion of one of India's richest financiers. The secretary, who was later placed in charge of a dam construction project, was afraid I might have damaged the illusion that Gandhi lived among the poor.

Gandhi preferred to keep himself in humble surroundings, but his sizable entourage of secretaries and other dedicated hangers-on took great pains to see that his comfort and well-being were not endangered. In the Bhangi Colony, where the sweepers lived, Gandhi's simple hut was fumigated, disinfected, and laid with carpets before he took up residence. He traveled third-class on the railroads, but what this amounted to was the allocation to him of a third-class coach as a private car.

Mrs. Sarojini Naidu, the poetess and wit, once commented to a correspondent, "The world will never know what it costs us to keep Gandhiji poor!"

It was Mrs. Naidu also who forced him to play pingpong

with her during one of his many imprisonments by the British. She thought it would be good for his health. Actually, Gandhi was extremely robust for his age and size, although his stooping walk, leaning on his two grandnieces, gave a false appearance of emaciation and weakness. His firm muscles were massaged daily, and his daily early morning walk was taken at a half-run that kept his younger followers gasping for breath.

Gandhi took the vow of celibacy while still a young man, but never ceased to be aware of women, as he was frank to say. Once a young man wrote him a letter, professing to be in great distress because he found that the innocent touch of a woman, such as a hand on the arm, gave him pleasure. Answering the letter in one of his open prayer meetings, Gandhi reassured the young man that there was nothing wrong with such a feeling. Not only did Gandhi share the sensation of pleasure in touching a woman, he said, but furthermore, he took every opportunity to do so!

One of the greatest news pictures ever made of Gandhi was taken at his meeting with Lady Mountbatten. As they moved away together, the little man in the loincloth casually placed his hand on the shoulder of the Viceroy's wife and let her support him as he walked. The picture, taken by Max Desfor of Associated Press, was one of the most discussed photos of the time, both in India and England, for such familiarity by a "native" toward the exalted Vicereine of the Indian Empire was inconceivable. In shock value it was comparable to the famous picture of General of the Army Douglas MacArthur, with his tie off, towering over the Emperor of Japan, published in Japanese newspapers.

Gandhi gave tremendous impetus to the emancipation of women in India. Long before his death, women were in the forefront of the Gandhian movement, and today many of the most active workers in the various welfare projects started by Gandhi are women.

One of Gandhi's legacies to India that the government

would like to have forgotten is the "fast unto death" that he used so effectively as a political weapon. Since India became free, hundreds of crackpots with grievances, and some who were not crackpots, have used the fast against their own government. Sometimes it even works. Once such a fast hastened the creation of a new state.

Potti Sriramalu was an aging Gandhian in the forefront of the Andhra movement to carve a linguistic state out of Madras Presidency for the thirty million Telegu speakers. As a final resort he fasted.

Tension mounted among the Andhras as Delhi continued to ignore the revered Telegu leader's refusal to take nourishment until his people's aspirations were satisfied. I happened to be in Madras on the fifty-eighth and final day of the fast, when Potti Sriramalu died. Thousands marched to his funeral pyre, and then, before the last embers of sandalwood had lost their red glow among the martyr's ashes, the whole Telegu area of South India burst into open defiance of the government. Railroads were sabotaged, police were stoned, and the rule of law was toppling. Within the week the Telegus were granted their desires, and in the course of time Andhra became the twenty-ninth state.

There is some doubt that Gandhi ever intended to starve to death. He was a master of the technique of the fast, and knew it. Once a lad with a grievance, who had undertaken what we might call a "wildcat fast" for whatever his cause was, wrote Gandhi to ask his approbation. Reading the letter aloud at his next prayer meeting, Gandhi was stern.

"Leave this fasting business to me," he said in effect. "Fasting is an art, and I know how to do it, you don't!"

In the last year of his life Gandhi's influence, particularly on youth, was waning. His real work was done with the achievement of independence, and now new situations were arising in which his parables did not seem to fit. Cynics were beginning to say that "the old man was growing senile," and to mock some of his metaphysical statements, such as his famous advice that "the first President of India should be an Untouchable girl." Remarks made for the ages were derided by introverted minds preoccupied with the narrow problems of the moment. The Hindu fanatics were outraged by his solicitude for persecuted Moslems, which was to result shortly in his death.

But the greater minds, such as Nehru and Patel, continued to sit at the master's feet. He was consulted on the Kashmir problem, and gave his assent to the use of the Indian Army. But he prevailed upon Patel to sanction the turning over to Pakistan of its share of joint assets, a huge sum, in spite of the Kashmir crisis.

The elite and the intelligentsia continued to pack his famous prayer meetings in the quiet, orderly garden of Birla House. His simple homilies in Hindustani followed a devotional period in which honor was paid to every great religion, including Christianity and Islam, through readings from their sacred books.

One afternoon, as the prayer meeting was beginning, a small, crude bomb exploded on the compound wall about forty feet from where the leader sat cross-legged on the prayer platform. Police wanted to increase the security precautions around Birla House, but Gandhi demurred. Ten days later, as he was walking to his place through the usual dense crowd, Nathuram Vinayak Godse stepped into his path, raised a pistol and fired three times. Mumbling, "He Ram, He Ram!" (Oh God, Oh God!), Gandhi sank to the paved walk, never to speak again.

When I reached the scene a few minutes later, the crowd was hushed, as if stunned. Those of us who got inside the compound could see Gandhi's still face through the window over the cot where he lay, breathing his last. Word of the assassination was spreading rapidly through the city, and the broad street outside was already jammed with silent watchers. Finally Nehru came out of the house and informed the gathering, in tones of inexpressible sadness, that the master was no more, and a "great light" had gone out of the world.

Even my own insignificant life had been bettered by the brief crossing of my erratic path with his, I reflected. Often, at the end of a frustrating day, I had recalled his twinkling remark on his last birthday, "We start a new life every morning." As Nehru said on the radio that night, the light that was Gandhi will continue to shine on the world.

20

The New Gandhi

GANDHI HAD A MAGNIFICENT FUNERAL, THE KIND ONLY THE East can provide. A million people watched the final procession through New Delhi to the bank of the sacred Jumna River, where his body was burned, according to Hindu rites, on a tower of sandalwood immersed in *ghee* (clarified butter). This spot, the *samadhi*, is now the center of a memorial park. Distinguished visitors remove their shoes to place wreaths on the plaque.

After the rites on the Jumna bank, the charred bones and ashes of the martyr were gathered in an urn, washed in milk, and conveyed by special train to the holiest spot in India, the *Sangam* at Prayag, outside Nehru's home city of Allahabad. The *Sangam* is the confluence of the sanctified river Ganges with the holy Jumna, and also, according to Hindu legend, with the mythical underground river Saraswati. While three million people watched from the sandy banks, the leader's remains were taken in a boat to the *Triveni*, the exact spot where the rivers meet, and there were immersed in the purifying waters. To a Hindu, this rite assures eternal bliss.

Portions of Gandhi's ashes were flown to Indian colonies in many parts of the world for enshrinement, while his own country lay in national mourning for days. Conscience-stricken, the nation searched its soul and vowed to cling to the precepts of tolerance and compassion taught by the father of the country's independence.

In the months immediately following Gandhi's death, the country seemed to be searching for a new spiritual preceptor. The New Delhi Hindustan *Times,* edited by Gandhi's son Devadas, as if voicing a national need, began publicizing the prayer meetings being held nightly, after Gandhi's own fashion, by a little-known disciple of the Mahatma named Vinoba Bhave.

Bhave (pronounced bhah'-vay, with a slight aspiration of the first "h") had left his middle-class home in boyhood to pursue the mystic path of truth, and inevitably had ended his search in Gandhi's dedicated retinue. The master, impressed with the young man's mental gifts, selected him for the honor of being the first to court arrest in one of the civil disobedience campaigns. In later years he became one of Gandhi's most trusted welfare workers, but he remained in the background and was hardly known to the general public.

After a few weeks of celebrity on the front pages of the Hindustan *Times,* Bhave again disappeared from view. When he next came to public notice, several years later, he was to electrify all India with a new idea, and become known throughout the world. The movement he conceived could have taken hold only in India, and probably only a man like Bhave, with his Hindu mysticism, his piety, and even a physical resemblance to the late Mahatma, could have led it.

Like many Indians at this time, Bhave—who by now was being addressed respectfully as *Acharya,* or preceptor—was brooding over the ancient curse that lay on India in its archaic land system, perhaps the most complicated and oppressive in the world. To state merely that too much of the land was owned by too few persons is to fail to do justice to the problem. There were almost innumerable variations of the basic pattern that kept land wealth in the hands of a small percentage of the population, while the greater part were condemned to a hopelessness approaching that of outright slavery, which in some parts of the country it almost literally was.

Vast areas were under control of *zamindars,* who originated as local tax collectors for the Moguls and later the British. The *zamindari* system, reduced to its simplest terms, made the chosen person responsible for all land taxes. What he could squeeze out of the cultivators above his obligation to the government was his. In time the *zamindars* acquired general acceptance as the owners of the land.

There was a peculiarly vicious variation of this system, almost incredible in the twentieth century, that obtained in many of the princely states particularly. In times past, ruling princes had been accustomed to rewarding services with grants of territory within their domains. These were called *jagirs,* and might be bestowed for valor in battle, for the composition of a pleasing poem, the discovery of an exceptional addition to the ruler's harem, or on any other whim of the prince. The *jagirdar's* land, which might include a number of populated villages, became his hereditary barony, in which he was the absolute power answerable only to his prince. The *jagirdar* often had the title of Rajah. I once met one such, in Jaipur, who told me that until recently he might, if he wished, have had me murdered in his *jagir* and be answerable to no authority but that of the Maharajah of Jaipur.

Since the land tenure system varied bewilderingly, so many of the hundreds of ruling princes having had their own special ideas of administration, reforms had to be left to the individual states. The aim in general, of course, was to give the ownership of land to the actual cultivator. The Constitution required that the dispossessed *zamindar* or his counterpart must be compensated fairly; this was a serious hitch that irritated Nehru and many others, and has caused Indians to look enviously at Communist China, where the totalitarian government is bothered by no such obstacles as owner's rights.

The solution found was to set a value on the land to be expropriated, and assess the new peasant-owner a tax from which the former landlord would be paid over a long period of years. This method, of course, provided little if any immediate relief to the peasant, who merely paid to the government about what he formerly paid his *zamindar*. And the *zamindars* and *jagirdars*, like the former ruling princes, had been both good and bad. Some were generous and kindly to their tenants, taking their peasants' troubles as their own. In such instances, which no doubt were more the exception than the rule, the cultivator merely exchanged a paternalistic overlord for the doubtful benevolence of an impersonal government.

Under these conditions, the government's efforts toward a vital reform were hampered by a lack of popular enthusiasm also noticeable in other fields. Nevertheless, it was essential that rehabilitation of rural economy be given a top priority. According to the latest census figures, 70 per cent of the Indian population belonged to the agricultural class. Of these, only 28 per cent were self-supporting. About three-fourths of the population of rural India was out of work seven to eight months a year, and the other fourth was unemployed for at least three months.

Indian economic planners knew that it would take many years to eradicate such conditions. Nevertheless, it was essential to initiate reforms at once. The *zamindars*, however, were not to be eliminated without a fight. A long series of delaying actions began in the courts. Meanwhile the peasants were becoming awakened and impatient for some of the benefits that they had been promised would flow from independence. The Communists and Socialists, both of whom were for outright expropriation of land, were making telling inroads on rural political thought.

While the Communists were running what amounted to a Red enclave in Telengana, one of the areas where landless peasants suffered worst, democratic forces in India suddenly acquired an unexpectedly powerful champion from the improbable direction of Acharya Vinoba Bhave.

Bhave, with a typically Gandhian disregard for conservative economic principles, decided that land reform through normal processes of law was not going fast enough. He decided to seek a remedy not in reason, or patriotism, or economics, but on the spiritual plane.

What Bhave conceived was his now famous *bhoodan yagna*, or land-gift movement. He planned to appeal directly to landlords to donate part of their acreages gratis to those who had none. Bhave would be the middle man, receiving the gifts of land and parceling them out to the landless peasants.

The frail, gray-bearded ascetic decided to begin in Telengana, heart of the Communist violent movement. Disregarding warnings that his life would be in danger, he gathered a few followers and started out on foot.

With his retinue of dedicated young men and women, serious, bespectacled devotees of the same type that always surrounded Gandhi, Bhave marched from village to village, holding prayer meetings at which he pleaded with the landlords: "If you had four sons, on your death you would divide your land equally among them. Consider me your fifth son, and give me my share now!"

In any other country, the thin, half-naked mystic would have been derided as an eccentric, and possibly arrested for holding unlicensed meetings. But this was India, a land hungering for another Gandhi. Bhave's simple appeal struck an immediate chord.

One after another, landlords stepped out with offerings of an acre, half an acre, a whole paddy field. When donations were slow in coming, a poor peasant would humbly offer a *bigha*, the tiniest land unit, one-sixth of an acre. Bhave would accept any amount. Soon the bigger landlords would be shamed into coming forward, and eventually it became fashionable to donate, and even dangerous not to do so.

Bhave and his growing band tramped hundreds of miles, through all kinds of country and weather, paying no more heed to warnings of snakes and tigers on their jungle paths than to the threats of the Communists, whose methods Bhave denounced daily as misleading and godless.

Soon the walking land missionary's movements were known far in advance, and every village on his route would erect arches of marigolds and mango leaves, symbol of good fortune, in honor of his coming. His arrival would mean a holiday in the countryside for miles around. Reporters for foreign as well as Indian newspapers began to accompany his walking caravan.

Bhave's relentless march through Telengana gave the *coup de grâce* to the Communists in many villages, where the people were already becoming disillusioned and bitter with the terroristic methods of the Reds who had posed as saviors.

By this time the *bhoodan yagna* movement, at first received with skepticism and humor in the worldly city circles, was a national sensation that even its many critics could not ignore. The campaign had gone so far, and brought in donations of so many thousands of acres of land, that Nehru decided that Bhave should be taken seriously by the government.

Nehru invited Bhave to New Delhi. The ascetic replied that he would come, but would not arrive for some time, as he planned to walk. Living on goat's milk, for he suffered from stomach ulcers, he had already covered hundreds of miles on foot. By now his eccentricities and self-mortification, like Gandhi's, were accepted with reverence as an evidence of sainthood.

While Nehru waited, the government built a house of bamboo and thatch for Bhave near Gandhi's *samadhi*, and constructed a graveled road from the highway to Bhave's retreat, in anticipation of a heavy traffic in visitors. They had not miscalculated.

On Bhave's arrival, there was a stream of officials to his simple headquarters on the banks of the Jumna. Cabinet ministers and others with degrees from the greatest universities of Britain, Europe, and America took off their shoes and sat cross-legged before the fifty-eight-year-old mystic, paying serious attention to his views. Like his preceptor Gandhi, he often spoke in terms that might have been dismissed as double talk in a skeptical Western environment, but which here were examined and found to contain essential truths.

His name now a household word from one end of India to the other, and beginning to be known to the world through the dispatches of foreign correspondents from many countries, Bhave soon resumed his endless walk. In Bihar, he contracted malaria. Today, with "miracle" drugs, curing this malady, from which ten million Indians suffer and a million die each year, was a simple matter—except that Bhave refused to have anything to do with modern medicine.

It was only after Nehru and President Prasad sent personal pleas to Bhave that he consented to see a Western-trained doctor and accept treatment. He was already near death, and the newspapers were running daily bulletins on the fluctuations of his temperature. It may have been recalled to him that Gandhi himself, who had also scorned medicines, had finally submitted to surgery when he developed appendicitis. At any rate, the stubborn ascetic finally capitulated to the pleas coming in from all over the country, and with modern drugs he was brought out of danger overnight.

Now Bhave's campaign had been taken up in a big way by the Socialists. Jayaprakash Narayan joined him, and was shortly to announce his retirement from active politics to devote the rest of his life to *bhoodan* work. By this time Bhave had collected more than two and a half million acres of land, and announced that his goal was fifty million acres. That is one-sixth of the cultivated land area of all India.

Many have remained skeptical of the worth of *bhoodan yagna* in curing India's ancient agrarian evils, and many columns of newspaper space have been devoted to thoughtful criticisms. It was contended, for one thing, that such a system of redistribution would tend to increase the already difficult problem of fragmented holdings. Furthermore, the economists argued that simply redistributing land was not enough; a simultaneous attack must be made on attendant rural economic ills instituting cooperative marketing, better agricultural methods, a farm credit system, and many other improvements. There was also grave doubt as to the efficiency of the land redistribution machinery set up among Bhave's visionary followers.

Finally, it was established that many of the land gifts, attended by wide publicity, were of useless, rocky tracts of no value for growing crops. Many of the *zamindars*, it appeared, were acquiring merit in the eyes of their neighbors and at the same time ridding themselves of onerous land liabilities by giving their uneconomic holdings to Bhave.

But *bhoodan* had meanwhile become a force in India with a significance beyond whatever it may have accomplished in land redistribution. *Dan* (gift) took on the character of a religious evangelistic crusade. *Sampattidan*, or wealth-gift, was invented for those who had other possessions than land to give to the poor. Well-to-do women, mesmerized by the hysteria that was beginning to surround the Bhave movement, would donate bales of costly *saris*, and strip off their jewelry and ornaments to offer at Bhave's prayer meetings. The final step was *shramdan*, mind-gift, which brought in those who could contribute to the movement through their intellectual gifts.

What *bhoodan* has done is to supply a lacking element in free India's drive to raise itself by its bootstraps. The element missing was public enthusiasm. The Indian had been accustomed for too many centuries to the lethargy of fatalism. Always ruled from the top, he waited for his superiors to take the steps necessary to improve the general lot. He had been brought up to follow the way of his father and his father's father, not looking for new techniques until their benefits were demonstrated to him by someone else. And finally, his religion taught him that what happened in this life mattered little anyway.

Bhoodan, like Gandhi's nationalist movement through *satyagraha* (nonviolence), fired the Indian imagination through an appeal to the spiritual side. It is an effort to mobilize for economic uplift the same mystic forces in India that ultimately proved too much for the British in the political sphere.

It has been said by many that *bhoodan* is a phenomenon of a kind that could originate only in India. It may be equally true that only such a mystic approach, mastered and applied first by Gandhi and now by Vinoba Bhave, is capable of mobilizing India's brooding masses to a practical effect.

21

Toward a New Society

THROUGH ALL THE EFFORTS BEING MADE, THROUGH THE BHAVE movement as well as more standard approaches, a bloodless social revolution is gradually but inevitably taking place in rural India, which means most of the country.

The ancient system of intermediaries between the cultivator and the government has been abolished by law in most states, and most of India is covered by tenancy legislation assuring security of tenure, preventing rent gouging, and enabling tenant farmers to look forward to the day when they will own the land they till.

It has been proposed, in a general way, that landholdings be limited to thirty acres for a family, with a "floor" of five acres as the smallest economic unit. A land census is now being taken, on which the government will base its eventual policy. However, it should be emphasized that the Indian approach, as guided by Nehru, is not rigid. The thirty-acre ceiling is frequently mentioned, but Nehru once took occasion to remark that if a farm of larger size were found to be prosperous and an asset to the community, he would consider it foolishness to break it up in obedience to an arbitrary figure.

Similarly, Nehru has made it clear that the government has no intention of nationalizing a private industrial venture that is doing well. I believe he said this in connection with steel, meaning that while future steel development in India will be strictly a state venture, there is no thought of nationalizing the efficient and prosperous Tata steel enterprises.

The February 1955 report of V. T. Krishnamachari, deputy chairman of the planning commission, has outlined the progress of land reform. Mr. Krishnamachari is one of India's ablest administrators, and his report is notable for frankness as well as modesty, as when he declares that "it cannot, of course, be said that good progress has been made in all states, but everywhere the problem is being tackled earnestly."

However, he offers these figures:

"In Uttar Pradesh, for example, the proportion of cultivating owners is now 83 per cent as against 10 per cent of the total before the reforms. In Bombay, cultivating owners now form 66.3 per cent as against 10.6 per cent before the land reform movement."

And he adds significantly, "Such figures, even after making allowances for slight differences in definition, indicate the extent of social change that is taking place."

In the same report, Mr. Krishnamachari includes a warning that "we shall need two more Five-Year Plans for results of real significance." But certainly there is significance in the effort being made. Imaginative but not unrealistic planning, along with a limitless reservoir of talent for carrying out those plans, form India's greatest asset, one so encouraging that it is difficult to conceive that the Nehru government's economic aims will not be realized, given time.

Certainly, in the drawing and execution of a national plan, India is far ahead of any other democratic country in Asia, including Japan; and Nehru, who is in a position to know, says that India is ahead of Communist China, too.

What is the Five-Year Plan? Krishnamachari explained it most succinctly in his progress report:

"Our plan is democratic. We believe that the people should make the plan, accept it as their own and make all the sacrifices necessary for its accomplishment. This is fundamental. It is part of our way of life.

"In framing the first Five-Year Plan, we had four aims in view. These were:

"Firstly, to rehabilitate the economy which had run down as the result of the war, reverse the inflationary pressures, build up the transport system and ease the food and raw material position.

"Secondly, to formulate and execute programs of development which will be impressive in themselves while laying the foundation for larger ones in coming years.

"Thirdly, to initiate measures of social justice on a wide scale.

"Fourthly, to build up administrative and other organizations which would be equal to the large programs of reconstruction to which the nation is committed in coming years."

Every visitor to India, no matter how casual, sees something of the problem facing the planners even before he reaches his hotel. From all the major airports, which are outlying, he will drive through some of the most abysmal slum areas in the world, where large families are crowded together in miserable shacks made of any material they can lay their hands on. Thousands, lacking even this crude shelter, sleep under bridges and in dry culverts. Outside the biggest hotels in Calcutta he will see the homeless, barely covered by their filthy rags, huddled together on the sidewalks, against the walls of the principal business buildings.

On the hundred-and-twenty-mile drive from Delhi to Agra, which almost every tourist makes to view the Taj Mahal, he will pass through a succession of dismal mud villages that, in essentials, are exactly like half a million others. Most of the villages have no electric light, and many of the residents cannot afford kerosene for lamps. Generally speaking, sanitation is entirely lacking.

The average per capita income in India, according to official government estimates, is just under sixty dollars a year. In a bad crop year, peasants are glad to get such work as digging wells, in heat of more than 100 degrees, from dawn to dusk for the equivalent of ten cents a day.

The ordinary Indian eats but two meals a day, often only one, and his average caloric intake is from half to two-thirds of the recognized minimum requirement.

There are no reliable statistics on unemployment, but, as has already been noted, three-quarters of the rural population is out of work more than half the year and the rest for three or four months; in the urban areas, employment bureau figures indicate that jobs are available for only one person in every five who is looking for work, while the labor market is swelled by 3,500,000 new recruits every year.

A third of the yearly crop of new job-seekers are products of the schools and colleges who demand "white-collar" work as their right, and preferably in government employ. This mentality, as evidenced in an extreme reluctance on the part of middle-class Indians to take work that will soil the hands, can be traced partly to vestigial caste consciousness, but largely also to the British educational policy looking toward the creation of a large class of docile civil servants. The British encouraged Indians to think that it was a fine thing to be a *babu* in a government office; the pay was absurdly small, but the *babu* was tacitly permitted to supplement his salary through petty graft. The result today is a double evil.

Professor Paul Appleby, who made an intensive survey of Indian administrative methods for the government, said in his report that the Indian government was one of the least corrupt in the world. That would be on the higher levels; there have been few major scandals. But beneath the top layer, down through to the lowest clerk, the scale and pettiness of corruption defies credulity.

I took pains to investigate this personally, and saw a customs clerk in Calcutta accept a bribe of two annas (five cents!) from an Indian travel agency man to give an import application normal treatment instead of deliberately delaying it. I am sure of this case because the application happened to be mine.

Such bribery, from two annas up to thousands of rupees, is standard practice in contacts with petty officialdom. But I would go along with Professor Appleby 100 per cent in his estimate of the high integrity of Indian officials at the top.

Perhaps the worst aspect of *babuism* is its encouragement of the bureaucratic mentality. Appleby was appalled by the duplication of effort and other inefficiencies that he found in his survey of a number of central and provincial government offices. As an example, he cited an instance of a simple document having to pass through forty pairs of hands before action could be taken.

Many Americans who came to India with the intention of investing in the country have returned home in disgust with the frustrations of trying to deal with the government on the most trifling matter.

The government was so impressed with Appleby's book-length report that he was asked to come back. Nehru, who once referred to New Delhi as an "administrative jungle," is determined that the government shall have its face lifted along with the other reforms to bring India onto a par with other modern countries.

Nor is the educational sphere being overlooked. Experiments are afoot in several states to overhaul the system so as to put more emphasis on agriculture and craft work, and less on studies preparatory to university and white-collar jobs, both of which are hopelessly beyond the reach of all but a microscopic percentage of the population.

No reform comes painlessly in India. In Madras State, where the class conflict is between Aryan Brahmin and Dravidian non-Brahmin, the latter are opposing the new educational system on the ground that, by teaching children to carry on in their ancestral occupations, it tends to perpetuate caste distinctions. But a complete re-examination of the entire school structure is well under way; it extends to the universities, which many critics believe should revamp their curricula to focus major effort on technical studies, rather than the classics.

The first Five-Year Plan touches every facet of Indian life. The core of the program is built around the huge multipurpose river valley projects that will supply power to the countryside and towns, and bring vast new acreages under cultivation. To make the primary benefits available to the people there must be thousands of miles of new roads. An adult education program is necessary to teach the peasantry how to get the most out of newly provided opportunities. And in order that the basic aim of the plan, which is to give every Indian a decent living, shall not be defeated by the fecundity of the population, a birth control program is included.

Contrary to general supposition abroad, the rate of population increase in India is no greater than that of the United States or the British Isles. But, according to the last census, nearly half the births are in families that already include three or more children. The net increase in number of mouths to feed is on the order of 5,000,000 a year. At this rate, the census commissioner estimated, India's population will reach 450,000,000 by 1969.

According to the census commissioner's calculations, that will be the absolute saturation point, taxing the utmost limits of the country's capacity to produce. After that, the outlook is for hopeless poverty and famine.

However, the government's birth control program was already under way and meeting with a surprising response in the limited areas where clinics had been set up. There is nothing in either of the principal Indian religions to prohibit birth control, although there are orthodox Hindus who contend, with Gandhi, that the only permissible method is abstinence. The practical minds of India, recognizing at the outset the impossibility of popularizing abstinence, allotted $1,365,000 to the Health Ministry to start a nation-wide educational project on the limitation of families.

Dr. Abraham Stone, of the Planned Parenthood Federation of America, was brought out to train workers in explaining the rhythm system, of abstinence on the fertile days, which even the orthodox Hindus could accept. Since the rhythm system involves counting, the problem of illiteracy was a special complication. Dr. Stone instituted the necklace technique, in which beads are counted off each day, with green beads, for example, indicating the period of infertility, red beads the days when abstinence is advisable.

The story is told that many simple village wives simply moved the necklace around at will, thinking that it was only necessary to have the green beads in front to insure safety. But to counterbalance that story, there are innumerable instances wherein peasants showed a sincere interest and desire to limit their families by scientific methods.

One social worker told me that two village men walked eighty miles to visit her clinic. An earlier supposition that the average villager, man or woman, would be either too uninterested, or disinclined, to practice birth control has been proved false.

Today India is, I understand, the only country in the world that has formally adopted population control as part of the national development policy. In recognition of India's progressive effort, an Indian women's leader, Lady Dhanvanti Rama Rau, was elected president of the world Planned Parenthood Association.

The fruits of the first Five-Year Plan, including as it does many long-range projects, cannot be fully reaped at once. The budgeted expenditures on the program to the completion of the first period in 1956 is only about four and a half billion dollars, whereas the Planning Commission estimates that about eight times that much, and fifteen to twenty more years of effort, must be expended in order to assure all Indians of full employment at a substantially higher income rate than the present average of sixty dollars a year.

This is not a hopeless outlook when the accomplishments to date are considered.

Food production, in the first three years that the plan was in operation, increased nearly 20 per cent, and made it no longer necessary for India to finance heavy annual grain imports at the expense of precious foreign exchange resources which are needed for buying machinery and capital equipment. Technically, it can now be said that India is self-sufficient in food, an achievement that seemed impossible when such a goal was first mentioned a few years ago. It is true, however, that this is self-sufficiency on a terribly substandard diet, and that the picture can be reversed in one or two bad crop years.

During the three years, new irrigation schemes brought an additional 1,420,000 acres of land under the plow. The output of electric power has been increased by 315,000 kilowatts; production of jute, the principal export crop, was raised by 1,400,000 bales, cotton by 390,000 bales, sugar 300,000 tons. Industrial output increased 30 per cent. Hundreds of miles of new roads have been built, the number of tube wells more than doubled, new schools erected all over the country.

Turning to expansion in steel production, the communications systems, and so on, the list of achievements runs into striking figures.

In the sphere of public finance, India's budget is far from unsatisfactory, the expected operating deficit for the 1955-1956 fiscal year being only $63,357,000, not at all a dismaying figure for a country with India's resources. The balance of payments position, which fluctuates with conditions of world trade generally, gives no cause for alarm.

Summing up the economic outlook, one could fairly say that the government of India is in a far better position than many others, but the people of India are still at the low end of the scale, struggling painfully upward.

The historic significance of the Five-Year Plan lies in the awakening of the Indian population at large to the hope of a better day, and the spurring of national ambition to bring the day nearer by concerted effort. The consequence of this has been the beginning of an economic revolution in the towns and villages. The community projects, aided by United States government funds and the Ford Foundation, have now reached nearly 100,000 villages, and by 1956 will have covered one-fourth of the country.

The Community Projects Administration and the National Extension Service organizations working in the villages are purely Indian conceptions, based on experiences with experimental village projects undertaken in the immediate postwar years. The American contribution, in foreign aid funds and the assignment of experts from the United States in farm extension work and other fields, is sometimes overemphasized in the American press.

The United States contribution in money, while vital, comes to about one-tenth of India's own expenditure, and the American personnel employed are a relative handful. Chester Bowles, who as American Ambassador to India took a deep interest in the community projects particularly and assisted their conception more than most observers, either American or Indian, have realized, agreed with Nehru that the more lasting benefits of the program would spring from the Indians' own pride of accomplishment, the feeling of having bettered his condition through his own efforts.

Nehru's convictions on this subject are the reason, incidentally, for his apparent distaste for publicizing foreign assistance to India's development program. The Indian people for too long have languished in hopelessness, willing to rely on others.

Today a new and exciting spirit is sweeping the Indian

countryside. The villagers and peasants are learning what they can do, and have been awakened for the first time to the possibilities of the human will to improve.

The apathy of centuries is disappearing overnight as the community projects extend gradually over the country. Farmers content with the implements and cropping methods of their forefathers are now clamoring for improved seeds, tools, and techniques as they see them demonstrated. And they have been shown that if the village needs a new road or a schoolhouse, one way to get it is to build it themselves. Strange as it may seem to an American, this idea had apparently never occurred to them before.

The result has been, in the past three years, a fever for improvement that threatens now to outstrip the government's capacity to supply the necessary advice and aid.

It is this new spirit, more than the execution of blueprints and the expenditure of large sums of money, that is remaking the face of India. Horace Holmes, the American farm expert who helped pioneer the extension program, tells how a population of several hundred thousand peasants was about to evacuate a certain district in central India, because the soil had died and would no longer grow crops. As they prepared to move, a government team appeared and demonstrated how irrigation and fertilizer would revivify the tired soil. The peasants decided to try again, and today there is an increasingly prosperous and growing farm community in an area that, in an earlier time, would have been abandoned to become desert.

The most hopeful aspect of India's improvement program, as one assesses the outlook for the future, is this national awakening, the slow discovery by the Indian people of unsuspected capabilities in themselves. This process has far to go before it assumes the direction that could make India a powerful industrial nation, but the natural as well as human resources are there.

India was passed over by the Industrial Revolution, but

she is in on the beginning of the Atomic Age. Her human assets include a number of capable scientists, among them the great physicist C. V. Raman, winner of a Nobel Prize, and Dr. Homi Bhabha, who has been chosen as chairman of the first international conference on peaceful uses of atomic energy. Given the power of the atom in addition to her human and mineral wealth, the possibilities ahead of India are without limit.

22

India's Foreign Policy and the U.S.

Prime Minister Nehru once pointed out, in a memorable private conversation with this writer in New Delhi, that the foreign policy objectives of India and the United States are exactly the same in essentials. But the two countries, he added, are trying to reach those objectives by roads that occasionally diverge. Any nation's approach to international problems, he explained, is inevitably the result of its peculiar historical background.

Viewed in this light, it seems strange to Indians that their country's foreign policy should surprise American observers. New Delhi's course in international affairs has adhered so consistently to certain basic principles, enunciated by the Congress party as far back as 1925, that India's attitude in virtually any given situation can be accurately predicted.

The four cardinal tenets of Indian foreign policy adopted by Congress in 1925 are these:

1. Opposition to imperialism and colonial rule;
2. Support of subject peoples and oppressed races in their aspirations for freedom and equality;
3. Promotion of peace and abhorrence of war;
4. Avoidance of foreign entanglements.

The relationship India desires with other countries was spelled out in 1954 in a statement of the Five Principles, as follows:

1. Mutual respect for each other's territorial integrity and sovereignty;
2. Nonaggression;
3. Noninterference in each other's internal affairs;
4. Equality and mutual benefits;
5. Peaceful coexistence.

So far, agreements to these principles have been signed by India with Communist China, Yugoslavia, and Russia. Americans have been inclined to appraise these pacts in the context of the "cold war" between the Eastern and Western groups of powers, implying that India has somehow sided with the enemy.

But an entirely different significance could be read into these bilateral declarations of India and the leading Communist states. India's anxiety to conclude these accords with the Communist countries, Red China first of all, might be taken to imply that these are the nations whose friendly intent toward India, in New Delhi's view, needs to be affirmed. On the other hand, India feels that there is no compulsion to do other than take for granted the democratic world's acceptance of these guides to international conduct.

And Nehru might have recalled, if American commentators did not, that in 1941, a few days before Japan attacked Pearl Harbor, the then Secretary of State Cordell Hull in a note to Tokyo had stated America's principles for the interrelationship of states in practically the same terms: inviolability of sovereignty and of territorial integrity; nonintervention in other nations' internal affairs; reliance on international cooperation and conciliation; and the principle of equality. The term "coexistence" had not gained currency then.

In an earlier expansion on the four cardinal points of Indian foreign policy, the Congress party early in World War II stated on behalf of the Indian people that "Their sympathy is entirely on the side of democracy and freedom . . . they have a deep-rooted quarrel with systems which deny freedom and are based on violence and aggression."

Following out this declaration, Nehru has stated his distaste for communism in the plainest terms. Of Communist ideology, he has declared that it is "out-moded. . . . Marxism is out of date." Referring to the Communist system of government, he has said forcefully, "I do not like monolithic states." When confronted with the attempt of the Asian Communist conspiracy to identify itself with the nationalist movements of Malaya and Indo-China, he stated with some heat, "Communism is the antithesis of nationalism."

Granting Nehru's sincerity, Indians find it difficult to understand how, in the face of such statements, he can be accused of being pro-Communist, or even, as some Americans have put it, "neutral on the side of the Communists."

India's stand on any international problem is determined, as it must be in any country, by her own national interest at the moment. Her approach to the situation, again as in any other country, is influenced by her national outlook, which in turn is the product of her history and environment.

The paramount motivation in India's foreign policy is her overriding anxiety that the world be free of war. Remembering the economic effect on India of World War II, from which she has not yet fully recovered, India is conscious that she is not strong enough yet to come through another such conflict unscathed, even if she were not directly involved as a belligerent. The result for India of World War III might mean the end of all orderly progress in this century.

If India's efforts to further the cause of world peace happen to diverge from the path to the same objective pursued by another country, the only alternative so far as India is concerned is to try to seek a conciliation of views. In the case of North Korean aggression, Indian and American views coincided.

But as to Communist China, India and the United States have taken opposing stands from the start. India recognized the Peiping regime because it is the *de facto* government of all China except for certain offshore islands, including Formosa. But Nehru has stated repeatedly that diplomatic recognition did not imply approval of all that the Red Chinese government did, and in fact he has expressed strong disapproval on numerous occasions.

Narrowing the China question down to the boundaries of Korea, Nehru conceived that the mission of the United Nations forces was to drive the North Korean aggressor back across the thirty-eighth parallel. When it became evident that the U.N. troops intended to cross that line, the situation changed.

India's Ambassador in Peiping, K. M. Panikkar, was warned by the Red Chinese that they would enter the war if the thirty-eighth parallel were violated. This warning was received in New Delhi, and Nehru passed it to the United Nations headquarters. The warning was disregarded, the U.N. forces crossed the thirty-eighth parallel, and Communist China did come into the war.

When the resolution to brand Peiping as an aggressor came up in the U.N., Nehru opposed it on two considerations. For one thing, he said, he could understand Communist China's anxiety as hostile forces approached her Yalu River boundary. Secondly, and most important, he believed strongly that the U.N. resolution was calculated to increase tension, extend the sphere of the cold war to Asia, and thus worsen the world situation in general.

Meanwhile, India put forward the formula eventually adopted by the U.N. as the basis for a Korean ceasefire. When finally the fighting was stopped, India was chosen as chairman of the Neutral Nations Repatriation Commission, and was generally praised for skillful and impartial handling of the delicate issue of disputed prisoners of war.

Since the Korea affair, India has become increasingly prominent in the role of "honest broker" between East and West. Nehru's advisor and special envoy, V. K. Krishna Menon, has shuttled back and forth between New Delhi, the United Nations headquarters (where he is India's permanent representative), Washington, London, Geneva and Peiping in attempts to find common ground for the solution of problems. In recognition of the impartial sincerity of these efforts, India was entrusted with the chairmanship of the international truce commissions in Indo-China.

Relations between Communist China and India were severely strained when Peiping's armies seized control of Tibet, thus extending the Communist sphere to India's northern borders. Even as the Chinese troops marched, a Tibetan delegation was in New Delhi awaiting permission to proceed to Peiping for discussions, and it particularly shocked Nehru that the Chinese should open hostilities when the means to a possible bloodless settlement were at hand.

Nehru protested vigorously to Red Chinese Premier Chou En-lai in two notes, but was told, in effect, that the Tibet affair was China's domestic concern, that Nehru should mind his own business, and that he was only an imperialist stooge.

India was in no position to send an army over the Himalayas to Tibet's rescue, even had she been inclined to do so. With the rebuff from Peiping, diplomatic resources were exhausted, for no country recognized Tibet as an international entity. Washington had previously declined to accord official status to a Tibetan delegation, on the grounds that the Himalayan state had no sovereign status. The United Nations similarly ignored a Tibetan protest over the Red Chinese invasion.

Being powerless in the matter, Nehru had only two courses open, and he seized both of them. One was to strengthen defenses along the Indo-Tibetan border, which he did at once. The other was to try to obtain reassurance of Communist China's peaceful intent toward India, which he did in the declaration of the Five Principles signed with Chou En-lai in New Delhi in June 1954. Confronted with considerable uneasiness as to the Tibetan development in the Indian Parliament and elsewhere, Nehru as a politician could hardly do else but to try, publicly, to rationalize the situation.

As a further safeguard to his borders with Red China,

Nehru cast a cloak of Indian guardianship over the independent Himalayan kingdom of Nepal. This was a step not altogether pleasing to the Nepalese, who consider India no less than China a potential threat to the little mountain state's independence.

Simultaneously New Delhi moved to buttress two other Himalayan states lying between India and the Communist realm. These are Sikkim and Bhutan, whose juridical status is that of "protected states," autonomous in domestic affairs but with India responsible for their defense and foreign relations. Each is ruled by a Maharajah.

Sikkim lies on the most convenient trade route between India and Tibet, with the road running through Gangtok, the capital. The adjacent state of Bhutan is the most exclusive country on earth. It is a ten-day journey on horseback to reach the border, over dangerous mountain trails. Few Britons, only one American, and not many Indians have been allowed in by the Maharajah. Both Sikkim and Bhutan are predominantly Buddhist, owing spiritual allegiance to the Dalai Lama of Tibet.

Two potentially historic developments have occurred with the emergence of a Communist government in China. One is the junction of Russian and Chinese interests on the borders of India, an eventuality that the British took pains to prevent through the encouragement of buffer states like Tibet and Afghanistan. The other is the growth of relations between India and China.

In all past history, India and China have had little in common beyond a limited cultural exchange through Indian Buddhist missionaries to China, and Chinese Buddhist pilgrims to the holy places in India. In recent times they developed a certain amount of mutual sympathy through similar experiences with foreign exploitation, causing them to share a suspicion of colonialism and the West.

It is only since India recognized the Mao Tse-tung government a few years ago that there has been a significant interchange between the two countries. And even this has been only on the political and cultural levels, for there is little possibility of an expansion of trade between India and China, both being have-not nations. Technically, there is little, if anything, that India can learn from China; most of what various Indian government survey missions have observed there has tended to confirm Nehru's publicly expressed conviction that India is progressing faster and more efficiently under a democratic system.

Nehru espouses Red China's claim to admission to the United Nations because, in his opinion, the entire effectiveness of the world organization is vitiated by the exclusion of a country that contains approximately one-quarter of the earth's population. He is convinced, also, that the only way to find common understanding with any country is to deal with her across the table, and he believes that the United Nations affords the best medium for such exchanges.

The fact that Red China stands condemned for past actions is, to him, entirely irrelevant to the current situation and need have no bearing on prospects for the future. Finally, Nehru finds it quite absurd that a government confined to the island of Formosa should be recognized as representing all China, and continue to hold the permanent seat for Asia on the Security Council of the United Nations.

Much of Nehru's apparent solicitude for Communist China can be traced to geopolitical factors. India, no less than the United States, is interested in keeping China and Russia apart.

Nehru once told me in a private interview that he believes there is more concern over China in Moscow than in Washington. China, he said, cannot be considered in the same category as the Sovietized states of Eastern Europe. She is far too big and powerful, he argues, to be anyone's satellite. Chinese influence is more likely to weigh on Russia, he believes, than the other way around.

Since India's chief concern is to see China independent of

Russian influence, it dismays Nehru that the United States should adopt a course that, as he sees it, is calculated to drive Peiping's leaders closer to the Kremlin. The attempted isolation of Communist China, by keeping her out of the United Nations and denying her access to Western trade, can have no other result, in Nehru's opinion, than to make that country more and more dependent upon Russia.

With Chinese-supported Communist influence penetrating into Indo-China and other Southeast Asian countries, India is far from insensible to a possible conflict of Indian and Chinese interests in nearby countries.

There have been indications for some time that a line has been drawn beyond which the Indians do not care to have Chinese influence pass. This line, corresponding to the boundaries of the Indian cultural sphere for ages past, encloses Burma and Thailand and bisects Indo-China. Vietnam, which Indians conceive to have derived its culture principally from China, is excluded, and the fall of South Vietnam to communism can be regarded by India with equanimity.

But no encroachment into the kingdoms of Laos and Cambodia, particularly the latter with its strong traces of Brahmanic cultural hegemony, could be accepted passively in New Delhi. And should Communist imperialism strike at Burma, it is a good bet that India would extend all possible help short of war to her weaker neighbor, including even the supply of arms.

Although Nehru is firmly committed against regional security pacts, tacit development of an Indian Monroe Doctrine for Southeast Asia is not inconceivable.

Nehru's horror of mutual security alignments, such as the Washington-sponsored Southeast Asia Defense Pact, stems partly from his policy of confining the area of conflict, and partly from his ingrained suspicion of any Western activities in Asia. Many Indians disagree with him on the question of regional alliances, and I would not be surprised if a different attitude were taken by his inevitable successor—if not the next Prime Minister, perhaps the one after that. But Nehru's distrust of defense arrangements between weak Asian states and the great powers of the Occident is deeply shared by an overwhelming majority of Indians, who see military reliance on another nation as an inescapable derogation of independence.

"A military alliance among the Great Powers has some meaning, but I do not understand pacts and alliances between a huge giant of a Power and a little pigmy of a country," Nehru told his Parliament in March 1955. "To attach small countries in such military alliances really and simply means, if I may say so, that these countries are becoming dependent and frightened themselves."

Once, in a private conversation, Nehru explained what he meant by taking the example of the Republic of Korea. "I do not suggest," his thought ran, "that the United States assumes the right to interfere in Korean affairs because that country is dependent upon America for its defenses. But America nevertheless is in a position to put pressure on Korea at any time, whether she wants to do so or not, or even wants to be in such a position. Therefore Korea, or any other weak Asian state that is dependent upon another for its defense, cannot feel herself fully independent."

As Nehru and other Indians see it, military intrusion of Great Powers into Asia sows the seeds of a new form of colonialism. Emotionally, the average Indian is bound to be against this, because of his long and sad experience with foreign dominance. Considering the problem in a broader context, Nehru has seen the formation of pacts of one sort or another followed inevitably, as night follows day, by a countermove on the other side of the ideological fence, with consequent increase of tension in both camps. Preparation for war, he argues, does not lead to peace.

Here again, the background of India's motivations needs to be considered. Having no great military sinews of her own, India is reluctant to place herself in a position that would invite the unfriendly attention of a near and stronger power, like Russia or Communist China.

"If Canada were a potentially expansionist power and incomparably stronger militarily than the United States," a high official in the Indian foreign office once told me, "Americans would no doubt have a more sympathetic understanding of India's attitude toward Communist China."

Furthermore, the cold war is still remote from India geographically. She does not feel, as the United States must, that she is on the front line. At the time, just after World War II, when Americans became aware of the dangers of the international Communist conspiracy, India's full attention was focused on her own independence movement. Immediately afterward and for some time, internal affairs occupied India while the United States was being forced into the center of a world struggle.

Thus, India's sense of urgency in the ideological conflict being less acute, she is able to view affairs with what others may regard as shortsighted detachment, and proffer advice that, in a different light, may seem naïve and unrealistic. It does not seem so to India, where the precepts of Gandhi still condition thinking.

Nehru's visit in 1955 to Moscow, where he signed the Five Principles declaration with Soviet Premier Bulganin, produced an adverse reaction in the United States that must have been wholly unexpected in India, for the Moscow joint pronouncement contained nothing from Nehru's side that he had not said many times before, while it did contain an important concession from the Russians.

In the clause of the Five Principles pledging "noninterference in each other's internal affairs," Nehru persuaded the Kremlin to accept the additional phrase, "for any reason, either of economic, political or ideological character." This amounted to a promise by the Russians to withdraw support to the Indian Communist party. It was regarded in India as one of Nehru's greatest coups against the Reds.

Indians are under no more illusions than anyone else as to the reliability of Communist promises. But Indian skepticism takes a slightly different turn from that of most Americans. Instead of saying before the world, "we don't believe you," the Indians murmur quietly to themselves, "we will wait and see." The effect is the same: nobody is fooled.

Nehru's so-called "neutralism" is a misnomer, as Indians choose to interpret his policy. It is, rather, a policy of "non-involvement," of holding an area of peace, uncommitted to either side, whose influence can be exerted in either direction to bring about greater understanding between the opposed blocs.

K. M. Panikkar, an authority on Indian foreign policy, explained Indian "neutralism" in these words:

"By keeping aloof from the controversies of the cold war, she has been able to build up a position of independence and, in association with other states similarly placed, has been able to exercise considerable influence in the cause of international good will. This is in keeping with the policy of nonviolence for which Gandhiji stood in his lifetime and which, broadly speaking, is still the basis of India's thinking."

It has been asked whether India does not feel an obligation to throw her great moral weight on the side of her fellow democracies, menaced as they are by the evil doctrine of world communism. Actually, the weight is there, in Nehru's many emphatic denunciations of communism and aggression through subversion. He assured the United States Congress, during his visit to Washington in 1949, that in any choice between right and wrong India will never be found neutral.

India reserves the right, however, to consider every international question on its merits. In a particular case, such as one involving Communist China's admission to the United Nations, India may decide that the United States is wrong and Russia is right, and that is how India will vote. She has often voted on the American side, the most notable examples being her condemnation of North Korea as an aggressor, and her return of disputed Korean prisoners of war to the United Nations command when the Communists insisted that they continue to be held pending a political conference. (In that instance India agreed with the Communists in principle that efforts toward the holding of a political conference should continue, but as regards the actual disposition of the prisoners she accommodated the American point of view.)

"We do not intend changing," Nehru declared in his foreign policy speech to the Indian Parliament in February 1955. "We have no intention of turning Communists. But at the same time, we have no intention of being dragooned in any other direction. We propose to go along the democratic path. Our thinking does not lie in terms of a great crusade of communism or anticommunism."

In an earlier speech, Nehru said he thought that if the Russian people had it to do over again, they would not choose communism. He has indicated that the only reason he does not come out with a forthright denunciation of Communist imperialism in Eastern Europe, the way the Congress party denounced Nazi Germany's engulfment of some of the same countries, is that to do so at this time would have no other effect than to exacerbate cold war tensions. Such declarations at this stage, he feels, would destroy any value India might have in the role of bridge between East and West, and is therefore not to the world's interest.

The areas of disagreement between India and the United States, broadly speaking, are limited to questions of method in dealing with common problems. The heat of debate tends to obscure not only the abstract points of agreement but also India's concrete services to the American cause, as for example her continued supply to the United States of the bulk of her strategic export materials like manganese and mica. When the problems disappear, the agreements will become more apparent.

23

Message to Lhasa

ONE DULL SUNDAY EVENING IN NEW DELHI, I REMEMBERED suddenly that it was possible to send a telegram to Lhasa, the capital and Forbidden City of Tibet. At that time, in October of 1950, the Chinese Communists were pouring armies into the Himalayan Buddhist kingdom, and the big question was what was going to happen to His Holiness the Dalai Lama, spiritual and temporal ruler of three million Tibetans. The Dalai Lama was then fifteen years old, and was not to assume his full powers for three more years. So I drew up a quixotic telegram to the Regent, Takta Rimpoche.

A month before Jean and I, and a free-lance photographer named Bill Donnett, had had ambitions of being the first Americans to fly into the hermit kingdom of Nepal, in the Himalayas between India and Tibet. Not exactly the first, because Capt. Jim Lassiter, formerly of the U.S. Air Force and now chief pilot for H.H. the Maharadhiraj of Darbhanga, had been there in his Dakota. Jim dropped into our suite in the Hotel Imperial one morning to say that he was leaving for Darbhanga in an hour, and that if we could get ready in time to go with him, he would try to take us to Katmandu, Nepal's Shangri-La capital. Bill Donnett was with us at the time, and in less than an hour the three of us were ready.

We tried repeatedly to fly into Nepal, but every day the jagged, snow-capped Siwalik Range was covered by a wall of white mist higher than our plane could fly. Finally, the three of us got to Katmandu on foot, the old traditional way, first detouring by way of Bangalore, more than a thousand miles south of Darbhanga, where Jim was having his plane refurbished. My itinerary must have looked funny to the office, if anyone there checked my route on a map.

Sitting at my typewriter that Sunday night, I recalled that Jim had expressed a keen desire to fly a Dakota to Lhasa. He had flown the Hump in the War, and knew the Himalayan country. He and I both studied terrain maps of Tibet, and were convinced that a plane could be landed on a flat plateau just outside the sacred city.

So I wired Takta Rimpoche, the Regent, that we Americans were extremely sympathetic to the plight of the Dalai Lama, that I had an airplane, with an experienced Himalayan pilot, that was capable of bringing out the young god-king, and of course the Regent himself, and other selected personages and possessions to the limit of the plane's carrying capacity. So would he please advise by telegraph to NYKTIMES NEWDELHI?

Telegrams probably never get to Lhasa anyway, and even if they do, the Indians will stop this brainstorm in a hurry, I thought. The telegraph line to Lhasa from Gangtok, capital of the Indian-protected state of Sikkim, was in India's charge, and all traffic open to scanning by the Indian Political Agent in the Sikkimese city. So I said to myself, Oh well, nothing ventured, nothing gained, but I'm sure wasting *Times* money on this wire. And as days went by I forgot the whole matter.

Exactly one week later came a reply from the Regent: "How soon can you come?" And instructing me to get in touch with his agents in Kalimpong, the last town on India's side of the Sikkim border, through which all Tibetan trade passed. I called Jim on the long-distance telephone—I hadn't bothered to check with him before, because the whole deal was too fantastic—and having got his O.K. I went to Kalimpong.

That was the wrong season of the year to go to Kalimpong, which is four thousand feet above the plains of Bengal, and is often sequestered by landslides on the one winding mountain road from the July rainy season until winter. But I took an Indian commercial plane to Bagdogra, the nearest airstrip to my objective, and then went by car until we were halted by the inevitable slide. I crawled a couple of miles over the tumbled earth and rocks, eventually got through to Kalimpong by telephone and had another car come down to pick me up. It was about nine o'clock at night, dark and bitterly cold, when I arrived at the Himalayan Hotel.

The Himalayan Hotel was a small establishment of about a dozen rooms, owned by the famous MacDonald family. The first David MacDonald was a Scottish clergyman's wandering son who got out of the British Army in Calcutta, made his way to Lhasa, and there married a Tibetan woman. His son, also named David, had been in the British political service in Tibet for some forty years before retiring in Kalimpong. One of his daughters, a tawny-skinned beautiful widow named Annie Perry, managed the hotel.

Annie Perry was regretful, but all the rooms were taken. She suggested that I try an Indian hotel nearby. After a quick survey of the soiled, probably verminous string-mattress beds available there, I walked back to the Himalayan and told Annie I'd be willing to sleep on the floor some place.

"Well, I'm not sure if I can do anything, but anyway, sit down and have dinner while I look around," said Annie. I had never met her before, but Annie had the hospitality of the mountain people.

While I ate, the Himalayan Hotel broke into life the like of which I never expected to see. The dining room and the lounge were practically one. A lot of people came into the lounge part, some of them in Tibetan dress, the men with their hair coiled around their heads in braids. A lovely young English blonde, who turned out to be the wife of David MacDonald the third, started a wind-up phonograph going with a samba. Then, as they say, the "joint started jumping."

Pretty soon I was in this party myself. The dark girl singing "Buttons and Bows" in the impromptu floor show turned out to be Princess Tess-la, daughter of a Tibetan noble from Lhasa. My first dance partner, the girl who convinced me that Himalayan women are the most beautiful on earth, was Princess Ke-sang, later to become the Maharani of Bhutan. Also present, besides two British correspondents covering the invasion of Tibet, were Prince Peter of Greece and Denmark, who was an anthropologist studying Tibetan lore, and an Irish Buddhist priest.

The Himalayan Hotel, whose front veranda commands a superb view of Kanchenjunga, the world's third highest mountain, gives the impression of being less a commercial caravanserai than a continuous house party. You come down to the lounge before dinner—during the day everybody is out studying Tibetan, or something—and play cards with the MacDonald family, gamble at dice with the Chinese Communist banking representative, or read by yourself, as you like. At the bar, you mix your own drinks and write your own chits. The evenings being nippy, on account of the altitude, the early sunset, and cold breezes from the snow-topped roof of the world across the gorge in Sikkim and Tibet, you edge close to a huge iron pot filled with glowing charcoal.

Old Man MacDonald, approaching eighty, would be listening to the news broadcast from New Delhi in the Nepalese language. The MacDonald "girls," Annie Perry and her sisters Vickie and Vera, spoke English to the guests, Hindustani to the servants, and Tibetan to Old David, who seemed to be most at home in that language. Young David, who was born in Lhasa and also spoke Tibetan, became our highly capable Kalimpong correspondent until his untimely death a couple of years later.

Foreign journalists were no novelty in Kalimpong, for that picturesque mountain town, with mule and yak caravans coming in every day from Lhasa with hides and musk, was the first source of news from Tibet. The only newspaper in the world in the Tibetan language was published there, the

Tibetan Mirror. So it was assumed that I was there on the usual mission. I did not tell the MacDonalds that every afternoon, when most of the Himalayan Hotel was having a siesta, I was slipping off to the residence of the chief of the Tibetan delegation to discuss details of the projected flight to Lhasa to bring out the Dalai Lama and company.

Nobody can procrastinate like Tibetans, I found. After a week of fruitless negotiation, the Tibetan officials advised me to return to Delhi, where they would let me know when to set up the flight with Jim Lassiter. To make the story short, it developed when I got back to the capital that the Indian government, as I had expected, had intercepted my exchange of messages with Lhasa, and had advised the Dalai Lama against the project.

The Indians had decided, perhaps rightly, that for the Dalai Lama to leave Tibet would remove the last hope of stability and resoluteness in that defenseless country as the Communists moved in. Eventually the young god-king, who was invested with full powers three years prematurely because of the crisis, did come by caravan as far as Yatung, the last town before reaching the border of Sikkim, in preparedness to take sanctuary in India if necessary, as his predecessor had done when an earlier Chinese government invaded his realm. Later he returned to Lhasa, still the nominal ruler under Chinese Communist tutelage.

Meanwhile, I learned later, the State Oracle in Lhasa had been consulted. There is a legend in Tibet that one day a lost kingdom of North Shambu-La will arise and conquer the world. Were the Communists, the Dalai Lama's advisors asked the Oracle, in reality North Shambu-La? The Oracle went into his routine trance and then announced no, this wasn't it, the Communists would turn out to be only a temporary nuisance.

Afterward, in New Delhi, I was told by Heinrich Harrer, the Austrian mountaineer who escaped to Lhasa from a wartime British prison camp in India and later wrote *Seven*

Years in Tibet, that a landing strip was being cleared for Lassiter's plane when the Indians killed the idea. Harrer wasn't sure that it would have succeeded anyway, as many of the powerful Buddhist monks opposed the trip and vowed that they would prevent our take-off with the Dalai Lama by covering the runway with their prostrate bodies.

24

Orphan of Nature

CHERRAPUNJI, THEY SAY, IS THE WETTEST SPOT ON EARTH, WITH an average annual rainfall of more than 400 inches, and a record of 905. The moisture-laden clouds sweep north from the Bay of Bengal, smash against the 4,000-foot cliffs, and dump their loads on Cherrapunji in raindrops as big as baseballs. The wind drives the big, hard globules of solid water horizontally across the fields and the small town, which is an important trade mart between Shillong, capital of India's Assam State, and Sylhet in East Pakistan. When the inhabitants of Cherrapunji venture out in this liquid artillery barrage, they wear strongly woven baskets of leaf and wicker, which hook over the head and hang down below the hips, so they look like huge beetles. The unhappy wayfarer carries a round wicker shield on one arm to ward off the hurtling drops, like a tribal warrior of the surrounding hills fending off arrows.

I had always thought of Cherrapunji as being a remote place where nobody goes, but while visiting Shillong, a cool, pine-clad hill station almost a mile above the steaming Bengal plain, I discovered that I could drive there in forty-five minutes on a first-class mountain road. This turned out to be one of the most scenic drives in India, with hundreds of feathery waterfalls spouting from the green cliffs.

It was not raining at all when I reached Cherrapunji; it turned out, in fact, that what is usually the "wettest" place on earth was, for the moment, one of the driest. For the rainiest town in the world was having a drought. It rains so much that little provision is made for water storage, so an unseasonable succession of sunny days turned out to be disastrous for a reason that the soaked residents of Cherrapunji could hardly have anticipated—no water. They had to call on the Army to bring in mobile tanks.

That was life in India, from one extreme to another. That same year I went to Madras to write about a drought, and stayed to cover a flood.

Nobody in the world takes such a beating from nature as the Indians do. Half the year they suffer hellish heat, and in the brief winter, throughout the northern half of the country, piercing cold takes a death toll from the thin-blooded, underfed peasants and city waifs, who can afford neither sufficient clothes nor fuel.

From June through September the monsoon winds, blowing onto the continent from thousands of miles of heated ocean, bring heavy rains and floods that turn hundreds of square miles into lakes every year. Thousands of mud-hut villages are washed away annually in the monsoon floods, hundreds of people lose their lives and thousands more lose their cattle and all their other possessions.

At any given moment there is a famine going on somewhere in India due to some natural calamity or crop failure. The government keeps sufficient reserve stocks of grain on hand, but it is a continual problem to keep the emergency stocks moving from one place to another as famine strikes now here, now there.

The prevailing hunger and undernourishment in India is not from lack of food in the country, but the absence of availability or, most often, of the money with which to buy it. The government cannot give the food away, for without reserves against the ever-present possibility of a major crop failure, the country would be constantly on the brink of disaster.

Occasionally, when everything else is going all right, there will be an earthquake to add to routine miseries. The great Assam quake of a few years ago was the second worst earth disturbance in history, eclipsed only by the explosion of Krakatoa. Rivers changed their courses, hills were flattened and new hills appeared, roads dropped out of sight, the whole topography of a vast area in northeastern India was changed. Fortunately, the historic upheaval occurred in sparsely populated country, so the loss of life was small.

It has been estimated that forty thousand Indians are killed every year by wild animals and poisonous snakes—almost one every fifteen minutes. Several years ago packs of wolves, hyenas, and jackals, driven from their natural lairs by an extensive jungle-clearance project in Uttar Pradesh State, invaded the great city of Lucknow, the state capital, and carried off more than thirty children. Babies were snatched from sleeping mothers' arms as the emboldened beasts began to raid nightly in the crowded slum quarters. One hungry animal penetrated to the better neighborhoods, and was discovered on the veranda of Nehru's son-in-law's residence. The scourge was ended only after the Army was called out and placed a cordon around the city.

A lone rhinoceros once terrorized a sizable town in Upper Assam for days. The great beast lumbered out of the jungle and had killed three men when the entire population took to their houses and barricaded the doors. The rhino methodically broke up a number of unattended shops, took a leisurely swim in the town reservoir, and when last seen was trampling through a tea garden. The marauder got away because no one dared shoot it without official permission from the state capital, far away. The vanishing Indian rhinoceros is a protected animal.

The sacred beasts of India are not only a nuisance but a huge drain on the food supply. Government food officials have estimated that the wild monkeys—venerated by Hindus because their ancestors, according to the legend, built a bridge to Ceylon for the god Rama to recapture his wife Sita from the demon-king—consume or destroy 10 per cent of the grain in the fields.

Indian officials, seldom orthodox-minded, recognize that the ubiquitous sacred cows are an intolerable burden, but all that can be done in the face of religious opinion is to make an effort to improve the breed. India has one-third of the world's cattle, but derives little benefit beyond the use of them as draft animals, and plenty of dung for fuel.

It always seems strange to a foreigner that the cow can be such an object of worship, and yet so neglected and mistreated. Emaciated cows wander at will through the streets of Delhi and Calcutta, fouling sidewalks, sometimes stopping at a roadside stand to sample the vegetables on display. They seem to belong to no one. The Delhi Municipal Committee rounds up stray cows regularly, keeps them awhile, and if they are unclaimed they are taken out of the city and released. Then they wander back again. Recently the committee had a proposal before it to cut the time of keeping the animals in half, to save expense.

Except for production of dung—which would be valuable as fertilizer, but is dried in cakes and used for fuel because wood and coal are expensive—the thousands of cows wandering about in the cities are worthless and destructive. But killing a cow, to a devout Hindu, is a crime worse than murder. During the war, in fact, American servicemen in Calcutta were instructed that if a traffic situation arose in which the driver had a choice of striking a cow or a human, hit the human and proceed without stopping to a police station. To injure a cow might be fatal.

Some communities have cow refuges, called *pinjrapoles,* to which old and diseased cattle are taken to die. A predecessor of mine once asked the Hindu in charge of a *pinjrapole* if it would not be more humane to put the miserable animals out of their evident misery with a merciful execution. "Would you kill your mother?" the Hindu asked simply.

Like everything else that's wrong with India, the cattle

problem is under government study. A campaign has been on for some years now to castrate the puny, defective bulls, and try gradually to build up a cattle population that will be an economic asset instead of a liability. The many benefits to be derived from maintaining good, productive bovine stock is, of course, the practical reason why the cow was originally placed under religious protection. Like many other aspects of Hinduism that once had a solid foundation in practicality or philosophy, cow worship also has been debased by superstition until the original purpose is no longer served.

25

"Spiritual" India

IT MAY BE, AS INDIANS ARE FOND OF ASSERTING, THAT RELIGION plays a greater role in the life of the people in India than in any other country. There are no statistics, for only among the Christians, who number no more than nine million, is there such a thing as formal membership in a religious group. The Moslem goes to the mosque on Friday, the Hindus and others worship as they see fit. The Hindu has, it is said, three hundred and thirty million gods. Actually, that is simply a number denoting infinity.

In recent years, it is understood, there has been evidence of a religious revival in greatly increased numbers of pilgrims to the great Indian Hindu festivals. This may also be due to greater availability of transportation facilities. At any rate, there is no doubt that the Hindus have the biggest religious gatherings in the world.

About every eighth person in the world is a Hindu. But all Hindus are Indians, the only exceptions being a few foreign devotees who may or may not be considered real Hindus, since they were not born into a caste; and the Nepalese, whose country is geographically an extension of India into the Himalayas. A Brahmanic religion is practiced in Bali, and Hinduism has exerted strong influence on the form of Buddhism practiced in Thailand and Cambodia. But since the Hindu religion forbade crossing the sea—the "black water"—a way of life grew up in the Indian peninsula that is unique in the world.

I have often wondered if this did not account for the fact that Indians and the peoples of the West so often have difficulty understanding each other's points of view. I believe it may have its influence on India's special approach to foreign policy, for example.

The *Kumbh Mela*, a month-long celebration held every twelve years at the confluence of the sacred rivers at Allahabad, draws five million pilgrims from all over India, by airplane, train, bullock cart, and afoot.

This *mela* recalls the struggle of gods and demons for a cup of life-giving nectar, or *kumbh*. A drop of the nectar was spilled into the waters where the rivers meet at Allahabad, and when the planets are in the favorable conjunction, a bath at the juncture of the three streams is supposed to shrive all sins. The broad ancient river bed of gleaming white sand, where the river no longer flows, becomes a vast tent city for the period of the *mela*, with circuses and all sorts of diversions for the pilgrims. At the last *Kumbh Mela* the rush of worshipers to the sacred waters became an uncontrollable stampede, and more than three hundred persons were trampled to death.

It is at this festival that one sees the famous congress of Nagas, the completely nude *sadhus*, who claim a privileged place. The Uttar Pradesh State authorities, who are in charge, make an effort to protect the naked men from photographers—not that the Nagas mind, but it is considered bad publicity for India.

I have seen nearly as many gather around the holy pond at Kurukshetra for an eclipse of the sun. Solar eclipses to the Hindu represent a re-enactment of the attempt of the demon Rahu, who was all head and no body, to swallow the sun. Kurukshetra is the most favorable spot for religious observances connected with the eclipse. Here was fought the epic battle described in the Mahabharata, here the god Krishna spoke to Arjun in the discourse known as the Bhagavad-Gita, or Song of God, sometimes called the Bible of Hinduism.

While the sun is obscured, all the gods of the Hindu pantheon are supposed to inhabit the holy pool, and that is when the pilgrims must bathe to insure life everlasting. The re-emergence of the sun is then hailed joyfully as the ultimate triumph of good over evil, which is the theme of all great Hindu festivals.

The Hindu preoccupation with the eternal struggle between good and evil, as exemplified in countless ways, may account for the frequent Indian assumption of superior spiritual qualities. The abject poverty of the mass of Indians may be another reason for continual loud exaltation of the spiritual over the material, even among Indians who spend most of their time accumulating wealth.

Perhaps also the consciousness of India's lack of material progress, as compared with the Western countries, and a national inferiority complex resulting therefrom, contribute to the state of mind of Indians who trumpet the "spirituality" of their country, always to the disadvantage of the "materialistic West."

As an American, belonging to the country that India considers the most "materialistic" of all, I was often singled out for special indoctrination on India's "moral superiority," and frequently in the course of seven years I got a little more than I could stand. At one time or another I was driven to the point of calling attention to the money-making propensities of certain Hindu castes, notably the *banyas,* and the morality of Indian business practices in general.

I could not help also referring, on occasion, to Bombay's infamous "cages," where thousands of prostitutes, selling their favors for as little as one rupee (21 cents), sit on display in block after block of cell-like rooms, gazing at the passers-by through metal bars like caged animals in a zoo.

I refrained, though tempted, from commenting on the ancient Hindu institution of *devadasis,* or temple prostitutes, with the obvious remark that nowhere in the materialistic West had I ever heard of a church keeping whores in the sacristy. (I should add, in fairness, that the *devadasis* have been abolished by law, though the custom is said to exist still in some places, quietly.)

In calmer moments I can find nothing wrong, and much to praise, in the inclination of Indians to view affairs from the moral point of view, if only they didn't talk about it so much. However, they are no worse in this respect than the American tourists who travel all over India boasting tactlessly of the greater progress and prosperity of the United States.

An American in India is impressed with the endless variety of the country, the continual discovery of unsuspected facets. Nehru once remarked that although he had studied India all his life and had traveled over much of it, he was always learning something new. In my seven years and more, few days went by in which I did not come upon an odd fact of which I had not previously been aware, or see some unexpected sight.

Somehow I was never able to make contact with the celebrated Indian magic, although I was always meeting people who had seen levitation, or some other marvelous feat. The nearest I got to the fabled "Indian rope trick," in which a boy climbs a rope and vanishes, was someone who had seen someone who claimed to have seen it. But I have seen yogis, adepts in the Hindu art of yoga, or muscular control, perform bodily contortions and other physical stunts beyond anything I have ever seen on the American stage.

Snake charmers were plentiful and sometimes revolting; I can never remember without a slight shudder the father-and-son snake charmer act in which the boy, a child of about ten, lay writhing in the dust as the father held a cobra while it bit the boy's tongue, bringing blood.

Some of the most charming interludes in my Indian travels were spent with the British planters still to be found here and there, raising tea, coffee, and rubber, often these days with Indian partners. The British, it is said, are doing more commercial business with India since independence than before. But the real old-time British types are not to be found so much in the great business houses of Calcutta, Bombay, and Madras as in the tea gardens of upper Assam and Bengal, and the coffee-growing plateaus of Coorg. There they live as they always have, since the days of Clive, many drinking their bottle of Scotch a day, often dressing for dinner though they may be completely alone.

I recall the sister of a British friend, married to a Briton who owned an immense farm in Bihar State near the Nepal border. On one of their rare visits to New Delhi, she related how the local authorities had "requisitioned" their jeep and car for official use in the elections.

"So for transport," she said, "we had to use our elephants."

"How many elephants do you have?" I asked, after thinking that over.

"Oh, we have six or seven," she said casually.

"But what," I inquired, "do you use elephants for on a farm?"

She looked at me strangely as if I were some inexplicable yahoo from the wilds.

"Why, for *shikar* [hunting], of course," she said, in a tone implying that surely everyone, but everyone, must have six or seven elephants on the place for *shikar!*

Many towns, particularly near the tea and coffee neighborhood, still have *pukka* British clubs where a traveler can eat, sleep, and drink, and they are better than any average Indian country hotel or rest house. Often they are quite deserted except for the resident secretary, usually a retired British Army officer living out his remaining days in India. The regular members come to town seldom, but never fail to gather from miles around for the "beat," held in February and October, just before and just after the "hot" weather. The "beat" begins on Friday night with a "cinemaw"; Saturday night is the "dawnce," and Sunday is for tennis and all that sort of thing, you know, if anyone is able. Monday morning they stagger back to the hills until the next "beat."

Most clubs now admit Indians to membership, or at least as guests, but there are some, like the ultraexclusive Bengal Club in Calcutta, that continued after India became independent to enforce the color bar. The Imperial Delhi Gymkhana Club in the capital city not only has a preponderance of Indian members, but knocked the word "Imperial" off the name, leaving only the Imperial Hotel as a reminder of empire (but it is Indian-owned, capitol of a hotel empire belonging to Rai Bahadur M. S. Oberoi, who rose from the humblest of clerkships to become the Hilton of India and Pakistan).

Looking back on India, I can understand why the old Britons are loath to leave, though they may curse the climate, the people, and the surroundings nightly over their *chhota pegs* (small whiskeys), as most of us have done at one time or another, including many Indians I know. The starkness of the country, even the rigors of the climate, have a grandeur about them that can be found nowhere else. The remains of great civilizations of the past lie all around, and there are some artistic and esthetic experiences, like one's first visit to the Ellora caves, which are vast temples carved out of solid living rock, that can hardly be equaled anywhere.

Both in its physical character and in its problems, the country is a challenge to the builder, the politician, the writer who tries to interpret India to the rest of the world.

In the part that the Indian people must play, they are rising to the challenge with their great gifts of spirit and enterprise. Everything in the world is wrong with India, in some part of it, but there is not a thing amiss for which a corrective is not being undertaken, from the modernization of the Hindu religious code to the bringing of modern sanitation practices to the ancient, sequestered fishing villages on the far Malabar Coast. And the tasks are being attacked with ingenuity and imagination, as well as determination.

Since, as Nehru has said, "India must run before she has learned to walk," some stumbles must be expected before she has completed her short-cut journey from the age of the bullock cart to the Atomic Age. On this leap into the future the old values stand India in good stead. Mechanization, for instance, must be one of the last steps in India's modernization. The latest in earth-moving machinery is used, of course, in the building of some of the huge dams. But on the same dams tens of thousands of coolies carry dirt in baskets on their heads, and it has to be so, for then they are part of it, and incidentally earn a living until the dam is built and irrigates fields that they can plow. India has no need for the photoelectric cell device that opens doors without visible human agency, like a ghost; India gets the same effect with a small boy standing by the handle.

Although India is new as a sovereign, independent republic, her tradition in democracy is very old, stemming from the ancient village system of popular government through the *panchayat*, or council of five. Building on this basis, the Republic of India today is the largest democracy in the world in terms of population. As such, she may well hold the balance of the future for Asia, and perhaps most of the world.

Index